Date Due

OCT 9			

No. 293   DEMCO-MADISON-WIS

STUDIES IN MODERN EUROPEAN LITERATURE
AND THOUGHT

General Editor

ERICH HELLER
*Professor of German
in the University College of Swansea*

ALESSANDRO MANZONI

ALESSANDRO MANZONI

BY

BERNARD WALL

NEW HAVEN
YALE UNIVERSITY PRESS
1954

CONTENTS

FOREWORD

It is many years since I first read Manzoni's *Promessi Sposi* and I have often returned to the book since. Yet in writing this essay on Manzoni I have felt an old uneasiness. How is it possible to present Manzoni in terms of clear ideas? Is it that deep down I am divided about him; that I admire him as a great European writer, and then at times feel that the grounds of that admiration are evanescent? Is it that in the restlessness and anguish of the mid-twentieth century Manzoni is too calm, too *enraciné*? Is it that we cannot place the book in the history of European novels? Is it Manzoni's virtuousness that is a barrier?

At least this can be said. We live in 'abnormal', unpredictable times, and Manzoni was in his writing always 'normal'. He was never *damné*, never scintillating, never paradoxical. His work was a work of common sense, of pedestrian observation architected to the level of genius.

There have been many misunderstandings about Italian culture in modern times, but the one about Manzoni has been the greatest of them all. I do not want to admit that literary taste is 'national'. Yet how explain that modern Italian writers who are most admired in the English-speaking countries, Italo Svevo and Ignazio Silone, have been indifferently received in their own country, whereas the admitted master of all Italian novelists has for so long failed to reach the extra-Italian world? Perhaps we can begin by taking it on faith that fifty million people cannot be wrong. We must be prepared to find Manzoni's work 'foreign'; if we expect it to conform to standards set by French or English novelists we will never understand it.

At times I have supposed that Italian is a language that does not translate, that Italian prose loses its savour in another language, that it is like those Italian wines whose bouquet we can only appreciate in the native hills. But I have suggested further reasons for the long neglect of Manzoni.

This neglect was only repaired in 1951, when the first unabridged version of *I Promessi Sposi* in English, done by Archibald Colquhoun, appeared on the bookstalls. *The Betrothed* was discovered by English critics. It takes its place belatedly on our bookshelves, together with the other great European novels that have become classics—and it still remains unique, unlike them all. I wish to thank Mr Colquhoun for permission to quote liberally from his version. And I ask the readers of this little book to get hold of it for themselves.

B.W.

I

Life and Times

It would be easy to describe the life and times of Manzoni if Italian literature were as well known as French. It is one of the greatest literatures, yet how many of the English or American travellers who go to see the Tuscan landscapes of the primitive painters, or the architectures of Rome, Florence and Venice, form a picture of the literary inheritance? They know something of Italian painting from Cimabue to Tiepolo; they have made their way through the rough ground of Dante and Petrarch, Boccaccio and perhaps even Tasso; yet I think that, all unknowing, they have an impression that Italian culture began to die in the age of the Counter-Reformation. Sacheverell Sitwell has helped to rehabilitate the great baroque architects, but no-one has given its due to Italian literature since the eighteenth century. Hence an almost insoluble problem. The period I am writing about may have been brilliant, but how am I to describe it unless I bring in names of writers who are little known or unknown? These names belong to a planetary system of their own. Italian writing, even to-day, tends to be 'ingrowing'.

Italy has profited enormously from never being 'centralized' by a single capital, but this makes Italian life seem a criss-cross of hieroglyphs to foreigners. One of the first questions we need to ask about any Italian writer or poet is what part of Italy he comes from. I do not wish to imply that all writing in Italy is regional; but when it is not it is usually European or cosmopolitan—one thinks of Casanova. Most writers are aware of what they have in common with others from their own city or province. Regions have had their ups and downs, but talent seems to have been equally spread, at least in the north of Italy, in the eighteenth and early nineteenth centuries. Amongst the Venetians were the writer of comedies Carlo Goldoni (1707-1793), and the poets Ugo Foscolo (1778-1828) and Niccolo Tommaseo (1802-1874) who came from Dalmatia and the Greek islands. Though the best-known Italian writer of tragedies, Vittorio Alfieri (1749-1803), travelled even more widely over Europe than Goldoni did, I imagine it would not be difficult to see something specifically Piedmontese about him. And both Goldoni and Alfieri are examples of another aspect of Italian regionalism—the question of dialects. For Goldoni wrote plays in Venetian as well as in Italian;

and Alfieri, like many writers before and after him, including Manzoni himself, had to spend some time in Florence to doff his native dialect and learn 'Tuscan'. I shall have to return to this point later.

Italy, then, has never had a capital in the sense in which London or Paris are capitals; but, at the time of Manzoni's birth there in 1785, Milan probably had as good a claim to be the cultural centre of Italy as anywhere. Each city or region in Italy has its particular historical character. The Milanese and Lombards became commercial at a very early date; they were bankers in the Middle Ages and they have thriven ever since on nearly every kind of trade and industry. Manzoni naturally inherited the prejudices of his fellow-Lombards. Though he belonged to the lesser aristocracy his outlook was what we should call middle class or bourgeois; for him industry and agriculture were creative, whereas war and high politics were destructive. Many Italian politicians have enjoyed war, but the mass of ordinary people are notoriously pacific. Violence is only popular when it takes the form of rioting, or hanging a tyrant, or fighting to defend one's home. Manzoni was born in the age of 'enlightened despotism', and the Austrians, who then ruled Lombardy, were in spirit paternal. By the end of the eighteenth century Venice had entered upon its final epoch of golden decadence, and Florence was the stronghold of an archaic pedantry in literature. Milan had more energy. Moreover the French Revolution and the Napoleonic wars were soon to turn Milanese society upside down. In a brilliant though nationalistic passage in *La Chartreuse de Parme* Stendhal describes the electrifying effect of the arrival of the French in the city. Under the Napoleonic régime Milan was awarded a primacy amongst Italian cities, at least after Rome, for it became the capital of the Kingdom of Italy. Ideas of Italian unity, thus fleetingly realised, were discussed with passion ever afterwards in the animated cafés under the enormous Gothic Duomo. Stendhal called this Napoleonic Milan the most civilised city in the world. Here Manzoni found a brilliant circle of friends or masters such as the priest-poet Giuseppe Parini and the chameleon-poet Vincenzo Monti, the Neapolitan historian Vincenzo Cuoco, and later Antonio Rosmini, the philosopher who was a champion of political liberty and social equality.

But I must not leap ahead too quickly. Manzoni, as I have already said, was born in 1785. His mother was Giulia Beccaria, daughter of a famous writer on criminology. His putative father was Pietro Manzoni, who seems to have been solid and dull and anyway was much older than his wife. I say 'putative father' because it is said that old Pietro Manzoni never really begot his son. Alessandro went out of his way to maintain that Manzoni was his father, and this is held to strengthen the theory that the true begetter was the poet Verri[1].

I feel the Freudians could make a lot out of Manzoni's illegitimacy. Worry about it may have affected his character. But more important, probably, was his parents' separation which occurred when he was a child. Manzoni's mother was brilliant and rather unstable. She became the mistress of a wealthy Milanese banker, Carlo Imbonati, and eloped with him to Paris. Manzoni was packed off to schools kept by religious congregations in Merate, Lugano and Milan; probably he felt bleak and lonely and, if so, this must have increased his natural introversion. The best we can say about his early education is that he was well grounded in the Latin classics, especially in Virgil, as well as in Dante and Petrarch, and that he learnt to love mountains, at least as a spectacle from a distance.

I mention his studies because they left a mark on his mind, one more permanent than the impressions of his later youth. It would have been extraordinary had young Manzoni failed to fall under the spell of the French *lumières* such as Voltaire and of Monti who was then at the summit of republican and anti-clerical enthusiasm. As a young man Manzoni sowed a sparse crop of wild oats, but his dissipation seems to have been half-hearted, especially if judged by the Italian standards of the time. His next step was to accept his mother's invitation to join her in Paris in 1805. Imbonati had just died and she was left alone, though she lived in the heart of the salon life of the capital of Europe, and knew the fashionable literary people. In Paris Manzoni deepened his knowledge of French literature and met some lions of the salons. But he was no good as a talker and made little impression personally. Some people admired his early verses and that was all.

Italian critics who have written about Manzoni are so numerous that there are many different opinions about French influence, from Voltaire to the early romantics, on his work. However this may be, we must not forget that there were two or three near-contemporary Italian writers who helped to account for the development of

---

[1] This opinion is defended by Mr Colquhoun in his essay on Manzoni appended to his translation of *I Promessi Sposi*.

Manzoni's literary ideas. One was Alfieri. Alfieri is best known abroad through his Autobiography. But this is mainly about travels, and subjects commonly associated with travel such as women and money. His tragedies are not at all what we would expect from the author of the Autobiography. Alfieri worked off his love interests in real life: his plays are 'noble and detached'. They are obsessed with the conflict between the oppressed and their oppressors, and the struggle of justice and freedom against the evil forces of power. Alfieri was an Italian patriot and at first the French Revolution filled him with enthusiasm. Later when the Revolution became cruel and mad, he expressed his disgust in ferocious anti-French poems. But he was a pioneer in that hatred of tyranny and love of the common people that we find in all Manzoni's work. Giuseppe Parini's ideas were even nearer to those of the mature Manzoni. He was a priest and also an ardent liberal. He welcomed the French when they arrived in Milan and participated in the administration they set up. As a poet Parini was inferior to Ugo Foscolo and to Manzoni himself. He is best known for a long poem called *Il Giorno*; it is a description of a day in the life of a rich and pampered young Milanese nobleman, as contrasted with the noble and hardworking life of the poor. Once again the leading idea is eminently moral. Moreover both Alfieri and Parini were in full reaction against the rhetorical classicism of the seventeenth and eighteenth centuries, and against the pastorals and shepherdesses of indoor men like Metastasio: and so they prepared the way for the so-called romantic movement in which Manzoni was to play the leading part.

In 1808, in Paris, Manzoni married his first wife, Henriette Blondel, a Swiss Calvinist. But soon after his marriage, he, his wife and his mother were all converted to Catholicism. His conversion caused a fundamental change in Manzoni's life and it had revolutionary effects on his work. His life was only creative in a major sense for about twenty years—roughly the twenty years that followed his conversion. His earliest mature poem, *In Morte di Carlo Imbonati* (*On the Death of Carlo Imbonati*) was completed in 1805. In 1827 he published *I Promessi Sposi* (*The Betrothed*). He spent the rest of his life re-correcting and re-editing *I Promessi Sposi*, composing occasional prose treatises, and managing his estate.

In character Manzoni was the very opposite of the hot-headed aristocrat Alfieri. He was neurotic and timid and, as we can see from *I Promessi Sposi*, he knew a good deal about cowardice as well as about moral principles. Crowds frightened him, so he did not play a very active part in the Risorgimento, though he always supported the cause of the nation. At first sight I find it hard to reconcile his neurotic personal habits with the calm, urbane spirit that breathes over the pages of his novel—the answer, I think, is that he overcame his outward limitations in his work, and it is there that we should look for the true, the 'great' Manzoni. He suffered from the cold and the damp of Lombard winters, and he developed a habit that must be unique in the long chronicle of literary eccentricities. He weighed his clothes several times a day, and increased or diminished his apparel according to changes of the thermometer.

Manzoni's fame grew with the years, but he himself lived more and more in retirement, either in his house in Milan, or else at his country seat at Brusuglio. His domestic life was unfortunate, for Henriette died in 1833 and he survived six of his children and even his second wife Teresa Borri Stampa. In his younger days Goethe admired and encouraged him. In his latter years he was visited by distinguished foreigners such as Newman, Gladstone and Balzac, and Italians made pilgrimages to him; but callers were not rewarded by any exhibition of brilliance. Gladstone wrote about his visit in 1838: 'I went to see Manzoni in his house some six or eight miles from Milan ... He was a most interesting man but was regarded, as I found, among the more fashionable priests in Milan as a *bacchettone* (hypocrite). In his own way he was, I think, a liberal and a nationalist, nor was the alliance of such politics with strong religious convictions uncommon amongst the more eminent Italians of those days.' [1]

Manzoni's portraits seem to me to reveal much about him. Certainly they show the difference between the writer at the maturity of his power and the monumental Manzoni. In the Manzoni of the creative period we see a man not unhandsome, with rough greying hair and a hint of muttonchop whiskers. His eyes have a calm gaze of awareness, but above all it is his mouth that is expressive, a timid and good-tempered mouth yet with irony playing about the edges. Then I think of the last photograph of Manzoni in old age. His alertness, his poise and his irony seem to have disappeared, the face is narrow and shrivelled between the now swollen muttonchops, and the whole air is that of someone worried and almost furtive.

[1] Morley's *Life of Gladstone*, Vol. I.

Il grande Manzoni is now a wreck. We remember that in 1830 Manzoni published his essay *Del Romanzo in Genere etc* (*About the Novel in General*) in which in the name of historical truth, he attacked the very principle of the historical novel, of which the *Promessi Sposi* is such a superb example.

Manzoni having outlived his family went on to outlive himself. In his old age he became a national monument of the Italians. His loyalty to the Church and to the principles of the Risorgimento remained to the end. When he died in 1873, in extreme old age, he was mourned as a hero of the Union of Italy; and Verdi, the other great popular artist of the nineteenth century, dedicated his *Requiem* to Manzoni's memory.

II

Poet and Dramatist

Manzoni's fame as the author of *I Promessi Sposi* has eclipsed his reputation as a poet. And this is as it should be, for his early work, seen in perspective, was no more than a preparation for the novel. Yet even had he never written *The Betrothed*, his poetry would have a niche in Italian literature. He has more power than Monti and more lucidity than Parini, and if he is surpassed in passion and in depth by Leopardi, at least his work, in its own different way, can be placed on a level with the melancholy moonlight poems of Ugo Foscolo, the author of the *Sepolcri*.

But Manzoni only wrote poetry for a short period. His reputation began with the publication of *In Morte di Carlo Imbonati* (1806) and *Urania* (1809). These works are of secondary interest because they derive from Monti and Parini. As I have already said, the Manzoni we know best is the Manzoni of the conversion onwards, and his finest poetic writing was the immediate outcome of religious inspiration. His new fervour was expressed in his *Inni Sacri* or *Sacred Hymns*. Four of these are dedicated to feasts of the Church: *Il Natale* (*Christmas*), *La Passione* (*Passiontide*), *La Risurrezione* (*The Resurrection* or *Eastertide*) and *Il Pentecoste* (*Whitsuntide*). The fifth, *In Nome di Maria*, is dedicated to the Madonna.

The religious poems were at first coldly received by Manzoni's admirers, which is scarcely surprising as they broke new ground and effected a revolution both in taste and in content, and in them Manzoni's authentic and unique tone was heard for the first time. In what does the Manzonian revolution consist? It is so quiet and peaceful that it would be surprising indeed if we got any impression of newness on first reading this religious verse—for the *Inni* look like strings of pious and conventional platitudes. And that is how many of his contemporaries judged them.

Here are some examples from *Il Pentecoste*:

> Madre de' Santi, immagine
> Della Città superna;
> Del sangue incorruttibile
> Conservatrice eterna;
> Tu che da tanti secoli
> Soffri, combatti e preghi;
> Che le tue tende spieghi
> Dall' uno all' altro mar . . .

> Mother of Saints, image
> Of the supernal city
> Eternally conserving
> The uncorrupted blood;
> You who through long ages
> Suffered, fought and prayed,
> You who pitch your tents
> From one to the other sea.

Manzoni's imagery is taken directly from the Bible, and the last line is a translation of the *A mari usque ad mare* of the seventy-first Psalm; but the stormy prophetical tones of the original have been lost, and an Italian lightness and limpidity have taken their place.

Or again, from the same piece:

> Campo di quei che sperano
> Chiesa del Dio vivente;
> Dov' eri mai? qual angolo
> Ti racogliea nascente,
> Quando il tuo Re, dai perfidi
> Tratto a morir sul colle,
> Imporporò le zolle
> Del suo sublime altar?

Field of those who hope
Church of the living God
Where were you and what corner
Was your refuge at your birth
When by perfidy your king
Was brought to die on a hill
Empurpling the clay
Of his altar sublime.

The depth of the feeling is half concealed by the extreme simplicity of the form. The best example of the same deceptiveness in
English is, of course, Wordsworth. Like Wordsworth's sonnets (the
best ones) Manzoni's odes wear well, and as we get to know his
verses better we appreciate that this simplicity is the outward form
of a subtle architecture. But we must not exaggerate resemblances
between Manzoni and Wordsworth. Italian poetry excels in vivid
colours and even Manzoni is inclined to see objects with the eye of
a painter.

We come nearer to our Manzoni of *I Promessi Sposi* in later lines
of the same poem—the Manzoni who thinks of the Christian religion
in terms not of ecclesiastical splendour or power but of the mission
to the poor and the outcast:

Perchè, baciando i pargoli,
    La schiava ancor sospira?
    E il sen che nutre i liberi
    Invidiando mira?
    Non sa che al regno i miseri
    Seco il Signor solleva?
    Che a tutti i figli d'Eva
    Nel suo dolor pensò?

Why, when she kisses her child
    Does the slave-woman still lament?
    Why does she look with envy
    On the breast that gives suck to the free?
    Does she not know that the outcast
    Are raised by the Lord to the Kingdom
    Who of all the children of Eve
    Bethought himself in his pain?

Or, a vision of Christian life:

> Spira de' nostri bamboli
> Nell' ineffabil riso:
> Spargi la casta porpora
> Alle donzelle in viso;
> Manda alle ascose vergini
> Le pure gioe ascose
> Consacra delle spose
> Il verecondo amor.

> Breathe in the ineffable
> Smile of our little children
> Spread the chastened blush
> On the cheeks of maidens;
> To virgins withdrawn from life
> Send pure hidden joy
> In the married consecrate
> The purity of love.

I have deliberately chosen to quote the most pious and trite-sounding lines. Do they not remind us of statues of the Sacro Cuore in Italian churches, of pilgrims singing sugary hymns and of lurid funeral monuments on which the virtues of a forgotten aunt are chronicled by the lucky heirs in words that end with *issimo*? Certainly religious expression in Italy has its tares, and tends to superstition, or to rhetoric, or to indulgence in a wallow of sentimentality. No-one could accuse Manzoni of the first two of these faults, but can we be sure about the third? It is not easy to make a judgment because Manzoni's softness or *morbidezza* is bound up with a virtue—with the kindly, urbane and optimistic attitude that he shares with the common people in Italy to-day.

The other religious poem that I have already called outstanding, *In nome di Maria*, is an example of his limpid and visual sense of the external world. The description of the Annunciation is weak and slight if we compare it with Dante, but it is as pure as water or a springtime sky:

> Tacita un giorno a non so che pendice
> Salia d'un fabbro nazaren la sposa
> Salia non vista alla magion felice
> D'una pregnante annosa.

E detto salve a lei che in riverenti
　　Accoglienze onoro l'inaspettata
　　Dio lodando, esclamò: Tutte le genti
　　Mi chiameran beata.

　In silence one day to some hillside or other
　　　There mounted the spouse of a Nazarene smith
　　　Unseen she mounted to the happy house
　　　Of a woman pregnant in her old age
　And she said hail to her, she who reverently
　　　Gave welcome to her unexpected guest
　　　Praising God exclaimed: All peoples
　　　Will call me blessed.

Manzoni's verse is not restricted to theology, but is always in-spired by strong religious feelings. He wrote an urgent patriotic poem, *Marzo 1821*, when he was excited by rumours that the Pied-montese were going to cross the Ticino and drive the Austrians out of Lombardy. Another poem, *Il Cinque Maggio*, on the death of Napoleon at Saint Helena, has interested me more:

　　　Fu vera gloria? ai posteri
　　　　L'ardua sentenza: nui
　　　　Chiniam la fronte al Massimo
　　　　Fattor che volle in lui
　　　　Del creator suo spirito
　　　　Piu vasta orma stampar . . .

　　　Ei si nomo: due secoli,
　　　　L'un contro l'altro armato
　　　　Sommessi a lui si volsero
　　　　Come aspettando il fato;
　　　　Ei fe' silenzio, ed arbitro
　　　　S'assise in mezzo a lor.

　　　Was this true glory? Posterity
　　　　Will make the hard judgment; we
　　　　Bow our heads before the Almighty
　　　　Maker, who willed through him
　　　　To imprint a larger footstep
　　　　Of his creative spirit.

At his name two ages
  Armed each against the other
  Turned to him in submission
  As though to attend on fate;
  There was silence when as arbiter
  He took his seat amidst them.

And then the last days at Saint Helena:

Tal su quell' alma il cumulo
  Delle memorie scese!
  Oh, quante volte ai posteri
  Narrar se stesso imprese,
  E sull' eterne pagine
  Cadde la stanca man.

O quante volte, al tacito
  Morir d'un giorno inerte
  Chinati a rai fulminei
  Le braccia al sen conserte,
  Stette, e dei dì che furono
  L'assalse il sovvenir! . . .

Heavy on that soul the weight
  Of memories descending
  How often for posterity
  He began to write his story
  And on the eternal pages
  His weary hand would fall.

How often when, in silence,
  The empty day lay dying
  His lightning eyes downcast
  Arms on breast enfolded
  He stood; and of the days gone by
  The memory assailed him . . .

Manzoni's thoughts about Napoleon were divided. On the one
hand the Emperor had been the herald of the movement for United
Italy, but on the other he was a supreme apostle of force and of war.
When Dante wrote of the after life of such men, he weighed the
pros and cons of their morality and, with what he imagined was
impartiality, he decided whether to send them to hell or purgatory.

Manzoni, the modern Italian, could not help bringing in the consoling thought of Heaven. He utters no threats or admonishments. He sees the Divine Pity coming to the rescue of the unfortunate Emperor—for like every man he had his point of view, and who can dare to make a judgment on him, *poverino*?

> ma valida
> Venne una man dal cielo
> E in più spirabil aere
> Pietosa il trasportò . . .

> a hand
> With power came down from heaven
> And in pity bore him
> To air that he could breathe . . .

I must now turn to Manzoni's two lyrical tragedies—*Il Conte di Carmagnola* (1820) and *Adelchi* (1822). Italy has always lagged behind other countries in stage drama. Goldoni and Alfieri, whatever their merits, are not the equals of Molière and Racine; and even the Renaissance, with all its power and brilliance, failed to develop great drama. Ariosto's plays are derivative from the Latin and written in an impossible metre, and so are rarely performed nowadays. The swiftest Italian comedy is Machiavelli's *Mandragola*. The failure in this field may perhaps be ascribed to the peculiar culture-pattern of Italian life. One wonders where the Elizabethan dramatists would have been without the Tudor Court and the City of London, and whether the French theatre would have been thinkable without Paris and Versailles.

Manzoni's tragedies are as inferior in dramatic qualities to *I Promessi Sposi* as Ariosto's plays are to the *Orlando Furioso*. They remind us of Goethe both in metre and treatment, and the comparison is damaging. The plots are in themselves powerful enough, but Manzoni failed to breathe dramatic passion and movement into them. *Il Conte di Carmagnola* is based on the life of the famous Condottiere, Francesco Bussone, Count of Carmagnola, who was employed by the Venetians to fight a war against the Visconti of Milan. The Venetians suspected that their Condottiere had betrayed them, and condemned him to death for treachery. It seems possible that the real Carmagnola did not always give his money's worth of fighting, but in Manzoni's version he became a hero. As important to the play as Carmagnola himself is Marco, the Venetian senator, who is torn between his friendship for the Condottiere and his loyalty to his State. Most of the details of the play are historically accurate, and Manzoni added notes which for the first time displayed that passion for discovering the exact truth about the past which was in the end to dominate him and to dry up his interest in imaginative writing and poetry. Manzoni also added a *Lettre à M. Chauvet sur l'unité de temps et de lieu dans la Tragédie*—an attack on Racine's *règles* and a declaration of romantic principles.

Immediately after the publication of the *Conte di Carmagnola* in 1820 (Goethe commended it warmly) Manzoni turned his attention to the theme of *Adelchi*. This play too is marred by cold and sterile interludes. The scene takes place at the time of the collapse of the Lombard kingdom in Northern Italy, and it deals with the struggle between Desiderio, the Lombard king, and Charlemagne; with the defeat of Desiderio and the death of his son, Adelchi. In writing the *Adelchi* Manzoni seems to have been even more preoccupied with historical facts than in the *Conte*, for besides historical notes he added an *Essay on some points of Lombardic history in Italy*. The subject, moreover, afforded larger scope to Manzoni's views about religion and morality. The hero, Adelchi himself, has a simple and Christian character, and he and Ermengarda, the repudiated wife of Charlemagne, are the more Christian in that their fate unites them with the oppressed:

> Te collocò la provida
> Sventura in fra gli oppressi . . .

> Provident misfortune
> Placed you among the oppressed . . .

that is, with the Italians, the *volgo disperso che nome non ha,*[1] the timid descendents of the ancient Romans who venture out of their caves and ruined palaces to see their Lombard masters fleeing before the Frankish conquerors only to discover that they have changed one *Herrenvolk* for another. Many passages in the *Adelchi* are (metre apart) in the style Manzoni perfected later in the *Promessi Sposi*. He had already attained his mastery of lively descriptions and of the use of a pregnant phrase for suggesting character. We find both in

[1] The scattered crowd that bears no name.

the well-known account of Deacon Martino's journey through the
Alps to join Charlemagne's army:

> null' altro
> Che i miei passi io sentiva, e ad ora ad ora
> Lo scrosciar dei torrenti, o l'improvviso
> Stridar del falso, o l'aquila del erto
> Nido spiccata sul mattin, rombando
> Passar sovra il mio capo, o, sul meriggio,
> Tocchi del sole, crepitar del pino
> Silvestre i coni . . .

> I heard
> Nought else save my footsteps and at times
> The roaring of the torrents and the sudden
> Cry of the hawk or the eagle that from its steep
> Nest plucked off in the morning flitted humming
> Overhead, or else the creaking pine cones
> That glanced in the mid-day sun . . .

Even more interesting than this typically Manzonian description of
Alpine scenery is the suggestion of character. In the mountain fast-
nesses Martino runs into a shepherd, of whom he asks his way.
The shepherd answers:

> 'Oltre quei monti
> Sono altri monti' ei disse, 'ed altri ancora;
> E lontan, lontan, Francia; ma via
> Non havvi; e mille son quei monti e tutti
> Erti, nudi, tremendi, inabitati
> Se non da spirti, ed uom mortal giammai
> Non li varcò . . .'

> 'Beyond those mountains
> Are other mountains,' he said, 'and others still;
> And then France, far, far away; but there is no path
> And those mountains are a thousand, all alike
> And steep, bare, fearful, uninhabited
> Except by spirits, and no mortal man
> Has ever crossed them . . .'

We hear the countryman's slow accent, we see his wide gestures
which are those of one who has for long been solitary, and the

expressions are imbued with the sense of the mystery that lies in the enormous mountains and in the unknown tracks. Indeed it is for passages such as this that Manzoni's lyrical dramas are best remembered. They stand by themselves as poems in their own right. But in relation to the drama they are only adornments and are extrinsic to the action and hold it up. Manzoni was a poet and a novelist, but he was not a playwright. And he only solved his problem of poetry and action, and fused both into one artistic whole, in his novel.

III

I Promessi Sposi

All Manzoni's life as an artist, then, led up to the writing of *I Promessi Sposi*, which he began in 1821. The first edition appeared in 1827, but he felt dissatisfied with it, partly on grounds of Italian style, for it contained many Lombardic and French expressions. So he turned his attention to the question of language, and spent a period in Florence to improve his knowledge of Tuscan and 'rinse his clothes in the Arno'. The definitive version of the novel was published in 1840–1842. Nobody, so far as I know, has ever disputed the superiority of the perfected work, which, apart from improvements in style, contains many interesting additions and omissions. I emphasize this point because second versions are often inferior to first versions—Tasso, for instance, ruined his *Gerusalemme Liberata* by 'improving' it in this way. It has been possible for critics to follow the development of *I Promessi Sposi* from its very earliest stages and thus to mark the improvements in Manzoni's craftsmanship. His latest version was very much more muted than his earliest; he preferred to suggest rather than to narrate, and he left more to the readers' imagination. He was a master of the 'work of the file' in the classical or Virgilian sense.

The opening passage of *I Promessi Sposi* is known to almost every Italian who can read. We are in *quel ramo del Lago di Como* ('that branch of the Lake of Como') on which the little town of Lecco stands, at the point at which the river Adda (which was later to matter so much to Manzoni's hero, Renzo Tramaglino, for in its course it marked the frontier between the Spanish dominion of Lombardy and the Republic of Saint Mark) flows from the lake

23

down into the plain. Higher up the lake towards Switzerland are tumbling mountains. The time is the early seventeenth century. Manzoni, with his scrupulousness about historical accuracy, is careful to tell us the exact date, 1628, and even the month and the day. The lakeside is dotted with villages. Some of them have not changed much in the last three hundred years, though Lecco itself has grown into an industrial town with chimneys. One of these villages is the heart of the whole story.

Manzoni's village is nameless, his hero is of the anonymous people; both are universal. The village is a village in the Italian lake district, one doubtless screened by Lombardy poplars and surrounded by the mulberry trees on which the silkworms for Lombard industry thrive. The houses are built of stone and their inhabitants are industrious. The women do housework, go to church, grow their vegetables and fatten their fowl. The men practise skilled trades. Renzo, as we shall discover, was a silk weaver. The village church has a Lombard tower and in the presbytery are the parish priest and his housekeeper.

As peaceful a scene as anywhere in Europe. But there is a snake in the grass: politics. In Lombardy politics consist of incomprehensible wars, the arrival of foreign soldiers, battles and depredations. In the early seventeenth century the foreign soldiers were Spaniards. When Manzoni wrote his book they were Austrians. There have been others since. But all alike brought trouble. In Lecco, then, there was a garrison of Spanish soldiers 'who taught modesty to the wives and daughters of the town, tickled up the shoulders of an occasional husband and father, and, towards the end of summer, never failed to scatter themselves among the vineyards, to thin out the grapes and lighten the labours of the vintage for the peasants'.

Manzoni detests war, he detests foreign soldiers, and he is on the side of the poor against the rich, of the industrious against the idle. Later, in a passage in which he compares the frugality of Cardinal Federigo Borrommeo with that of the austere Republicans of ancient Rome, Manzoni asks why the bread and water of the Cardinal never won him glory, and answers: 'Because Cardinal Federigo never killed anyone . . . If that morsel of bread had been eaten by a general in the presence of twenty thousand corpses, it would be put into all speeches and books . . .' Manzoni's critical weapon is irony. The Italians, unlike the Spaniards, are not an ironical people, and their literature has few examples of this mood—when Dante tries to be ironical he is invariably heavy-handed—and hence some critics have suggested that Manzoni owed his manner to Voltaire. But I think it would be easy to exaggerate this point. Manzoni's irony is no more that of Voltaire than it is that of Cervantes. Usually it is gentle and affectionate, and sometimes it is almost Chinese in its delicate *nuances*.

Don Abbondio, the parish priest of our village, is walking home along a hillside pass towards the evening of November 7th, 1628.

> He was calmly saying his office, every now and again, between one psalm and another, closing his breviary and leaving the index finger of his right hand in it as a bookmarker. Then he would put his other hand behind his back and with one foot kick away towards the wall the flints which littered the path; then raise his head, let his eye walk idly round and come to rest on a hillside which the rays of the setting sun, shining through the clefts of the opposite slope, were dappling with large irregular splashes of purple light here and there on the outstanding bluffs. After which he opened his breviary again and recited another verse, and so came to a turn of the path where he was in the habit of raising his eyes and glancing ahead of him; he did the same that day . . .

Notice the typical enumeration of visible details. Manzoni tells us what Don Abbondio did with his fingers, where he put his feet, where the sun was shining, how the path lay, and so on. This technique is a technique of painters, and we find it, in a form even more pronounced, in Dante's descriptions of hell or purgatory. It is the exact opposite of the technique of Dostoevsky whose people, even in a drawing-room, are like gyrating souls, thoughts, nerves, but without bodies.

But poor Don Abbondio. By the corner of the path along which he must pass, the priest espies two bravoes and they accost him. Lombardy at that time was swarming with bravoes—men whose modern counterparts are gangsters and black-marketeers. These particular bravoes are in the service of Don Rodrigo, a minor local boss who has set his mind on abducting Lucia Mondella, one of the girls of the parish. Now Lucia is already betrothed to Renzo Tramaglino, the young weaver, and Don Abbondio has already promised to perform the ceremony of marriage. The bravoes warn Don Abbondio, with threats, against marrying the couple.

Now Don Abbondio lacks what Eric Linklater's Private Angelo calls 'the gift of courage'; or, to use Manzoni's words, 'he was not born with the heart of a lion. From his earliest youth he had observed that in those times no-one was in a more awkward situation than an animal without tusks or claws, who yet was reluctant to be devoured'. Of course Lombardy did not lack laws, and very complicated ones, for punishing the guilty and protecting the innocent, but, as often happens, they only applied when the innocent were rich and power-ful and the guilty were poor or weak. Don Abbondio, who belongs to the second category of persons, takes counsel, as always, with his housekeeper, Perpetua. Perpetua, we realise, is a very competent housekeeper, for she knows all the rules for getting to heaven though not at the expense of practical sense about money and so on. Monopolising her priest is her life work. She advises Don Abbondio to seek the protection of the Archbishop, who is an even bigger fish than Don Rodrigo. Don Abbondio's reaction is immediate: 'Be quiet, will you? Be quiet, will you? Do you think that's the kind of advice to give a poor man like me? When I might get a musket shot in the back . . . God save us! Could the Archbishop put that right?'

Indeed, Don Abbondio is so frightened that he is not only un-dignified—which worries him little—he is even foolish. Perpetua has the common sense, the cunning, of the poor, and as she rightly answers: 'Oh, bullets aren't thrown about like sweets at a wedding; things would be in a bad way if these dogs bit every time they barked!' (I have heard this saying repeated almost word for word as a comment on a speech by Mussolini.)

But however this may be, the crisis develops when, on the follow-ing day, Renzo Tramaglino, in his Sunday suit and feathered hat, calls on Don Abbondio to discuss final points about his imminent marriage. Don Abbondio has recourse to the well-known ruse of feigning ignorance of the arrangement and of tangling up the simple young man with Latin words that are above his head. Renzo, like other people in the book, is much impressed by phrases in Latin (your *latinorum*, he calls it); but, simple though he is, his instinct soon tells him that he is being cheated, and his sense of justice outraged makes him lose his temper. The priest, who now as always would like to please everybody, is sufficiently frightened to promise to re-move 'the impediments' soon, while planning in his heart to play for time until Advent, when no marriages can be performed. Still further pressed he reveals the threats of Don Rodrigo. Renzo storms out, and Don Abbondio, quaking with fright, retires to bed. Per-petua announces that he has a fever.

Renzo, his promised bride Lucia, and Lucia's mother Agnese, now hold a council of war. Agnese is a match for Perpetua. Like Perpetua she has led a life of toil, and she is cynical about the powers that be. Like Perpetua she expresses herself in an idiom so peculiarly Italian in its *nuances* that it is hardly translatable into any other language. 'Don't be surprised,' as Agnese says on a later occasion: 'when you've known the world as long as I have, you'll realise that things aren't to be wondered at. All the gentry are a bit crazy. The best thing to do is to let them talk as they want, particularly if one needs them. Just look as if you're listening to them seriously, as if they were talking sense . . .' Stendhal also understood this Italian cynicism, though he never saw it from the point of view of the streets and fields. It is, after all, Count Mosca's advice in the *Chartreuse de Parme*: 'Believe or not, as you choose, what they teach you, but *never raise any objection*. Imagine they are teaching you the rules of the game of whist. Would you raise any objection to the rules of whist? And once you knew and had adopted those rules, would you not wish to win?' It is by a certain deceit that Italians have fought for and defended their liberty for a thousand years. I say a thousand years because it is only for bookish historians that Italian liberty came with the French Revolution and the Risorgimento. It always existed, under the Spaniards and Austrians, as under the Bourbons or Mussolini. Italian liberty is not a public achievement based on freedom of the press and honest law courts. It is a private achievement that one tries to make foolproof against the State. Agnese takes it for granted that the authorities are the enemies of poor people. Therefore poor people who have any sense must find a way round the law imposed by the authorities.

Manzoni was a liberal; he believed in public freedom, but he understood private freedom also. Agnese advises Renzo to discuss with the dishonest lawyer of Lecco, Dr Azzecca-Garbugli, or Quibble-Weaver, to see if he can think of a clever and dishonest plan. 'Go to Lecco, ask for Dr Quibble-Weaver and tell him . . . But don't go and call him that, for Heaven's sake, it's a nickname. You must say Dr . . . What's his name now? Oh dear, I don't know his real name; everyone calls him that. I've seen many a person in more of a mess than a chick in tar, and after an hour in private with Dr Quibble-Weaver (be very careful not to call him that, though) I've seen them, I tell you, cracking jokes about it.'

But unfortunately, Quibble-Weaver, though clever and dishonest, represents the kind of law that is the enemy of all the Tramaglinos and Mondellas of Italy, as Renzo discovers when he calls on him. The lawyer reels off wordy decrees about bravoes, decrees as turgid as modern income-tax forms, but he brings out the full savour of each phrase, Renzo is impressed. But Quibble-Weaver is convinced that Renzo is himself a bravo in trouble and he urges a complete confession: 'We shan't get anywhere. If you don't trust me we shan't get anywhere. You see, son, the man who tells lies to his lawyer is the kind of fool who would tell the truth to the judge. A lawyer must be told things frankly; then it's our job to muddle them up afterwards.' And, thus urged, Renzo blurts out the unpalatable truth, and explains that he is not a bravo at all, but a poor lad persecuted by the rich Don Rodrigo who is Quibble-Weaver's patron. The lawyer immediately abandons his learned citations and throws the young man out of his house with a mixture of fury and fear.

While Renzo is conferring with the lawyer, Agnese and Lucia have got into touch with the Capuchin friars, who in *I Promessi Sposi* are the friends and protectors of the unfortunate, and have found a pillar in the good Fra Cristofero. Manzoni's portraits of priests have been criticised from two opposite points of view. The clericals thought it was wrong of him to portray a priest as cowardly as Don Abbondio—I shall come in due course to the more important episode of the Nun of Monza—while the anti-clericals found Manzoni's piety at times unendurable; the poet Carducci said that he felt like throwing the book away. Both sides, it seems to me, were carried away by party passions. Manzoni's concern was to represent the truth, *il vero*.

Manzoni devotes a whole chapter to the background and life of Fra Cristofero who (like the founder of his order, San Francesco) was the son of a rich tradesman and had lived in luxury, surrounded by sycophants, until one day he killed a nobleman in a quarrel; whereupon he took sanctuary in a convent and ate the bread of humility. This chapter reminds me of Boccaccio. It is a brilliant short story in itself, a polished *intaglio*, and no other Italian prose writer is capable of such condensation or of such vivid and visual narration. But, to return to the story: we are brought to realise that, for all his years of discalced humility, Fra Cristofero has not lost the fire of his character. He visits Don Rodrigo in his vulture's nest, to appeal to him. He finds him drinking in the company of his cousin, Count Attilio, who is fashionable and rather effete and has a trace of the character of Sir Andrew Aguecheek. Don Rodrigo turns down Cristofero's appeal and the friar, forgetting for a moment that he is a Capuchin, loses his temper and threatens the nobleman. Then recollecting himself he 'turns his eyes to heaven'.

This is not the only occasion upon which Fra Cristofero turns his eyes to heaven and the action, like the blushes that suffuse Lucia's face every time marriage is mentioned, are as disconcerting to the modern reader as certain passages of Manzoni's religious verse to which I have already referred. Tartuffe, at least as performed by Louis Jouvet, turned his eyes to heaven. Indeed, if a living person 'turns his eyes to heaven' not only is our astronomy offended but we suspect the hypocrite or the pharisee. I remain with my suspicion that Manzoni is a trifle complacent about the sentimental pieties of popular religion, and I understand why some of his contemporaries called him a *bacchettone*. Yet these gestures in question are only repulsive because they are not spontaneous and whole-hearted. If they could be imagined as quite spontaneous and unselfconscious, as doubtless they were in the seventeenth century, then Manzoni is excused. We must adapt ourselves to his idiom rather than attempt to adapt his idiom to ourselves.

When he sees that it is no use appealing to Don Rodrigo's better nature because Don Rodrigo has not got one, Fra Cristofero plans to help Renzo and Lucia to flee to sanctuary. But meanwhile Agnese has thought out a more worldly plan. If the couple can somehow introduce themselves into Don Abbondio's house with witnesses, and declare before the priest that they are man and wife, then they will be validly married. The plan must be acted upon immediately because bravoes are prowling round the district like wolves. Another obstacle consists in Perpetua's vigilance. While the couple and their witnesses are penetrating the presbytery, Agnese has a grand battle of wits with Perpetua which takes the form of a conversation in which all the cunning of all the generations of peasants is brought into play. The witnesses, Renzo and Lucia track Don Abbondio to his upstairs room. But as soon as he espies the couple, and before they can pronounce the canonical words, Don Abbondio flees like a hare and begins rousing the whole village.

The three, Agnese, Renzo and Lucia, must now take to their heels in good earnest. They find momentary sanctuary in Fra Cristofero's convent at Pescarenico. From there Fra Cristofero dispatches Renzo to Milan, and Agnese and Lucia to a convent of Benedictine nuns in Monza.

Now there follows another of Manzoni's 'Boccaccian' interludes

—a story even more remarkable than that of Fra Cristofero. Power in the convent at Monza lies in the hands of La Signora, or 'the Lady' as she is called in the city, a personality whose ambiguous and intimate questions puzzle the simple Lucia and make her uneasy at the outset. Manzoni devotes many pages to a description of the background of this young nun. She is the daughter of a Milanese prince and her father has used all the moral pressure of their feudal family to cajole her to take the veil.

The unhappy creature of our story was still hidden in her mother's womb when her state in life had already been irrevocably settled. All that remained to be decided was whether it was to be a monk or a nun, a decision for which her presence, but not her consent, was required . . . On her seeing the light of day . . . dolls, dressed as nuns, were the first toys to be put into her hands, then holy pictures representing nuns . . . When the prince or the princess or the heir— the only male child to be brought up at home—wanted to express how well the child was looking, they seemed only able to express what they felt by saying: 'What a mother abbess!'

The story of the girl's struggles in the web of bigotry and hypocrisy, if read apart from its context in the novel, would stand beside Diderot's *La Religieuse* or the episodes of Julien Sorel's seminary life in *Le Rouge et le Noir*. The *nuances* of the psychology seem by their detail to be ahead of the age, and as though a prefiguration of Marcel Proust. Of course the girl, Gertrude, takes the veil. But she also takes a lover, Egidio, and is obliged to connive at a murder, committed to conceal their intimacy.

At this point we leave Lucia and accompany Renzo who is now entering Milan. In the early seventeenth century Milan consisted of only a ring of buildings centred round the Duomo, but then as now it was a beehive of industrious activity. Renzo—the *montanaro* or mountaineer as Manzoni calls him—wanders through busy streets as apprehensively as a nervous deer, seeking the Capuchin convent and the Fra Bonaventura to whom Fra Cristofero's letter of introduction is addressed.

It was a time of unsettlement and rioting. The immediate cause of the crisis in Milan was bread. There had been bad harvests, and 'the ravages and wastage of war (that glorious war we have mentioned above) were such that many more farms than usual in the part of the country nearest the fighting were abandoned and left untilled by the peasants . . .' Manzoni takes pains with the practical details of economy. People have forgotten about the bad harvests. They believe that the shortage is due to guilty men who hoard flour. Moreover the Spanish Grand Chancellor, Antonio Ferrer, has been experimenting in *dirigismo* or State intervention, and has lowered the maximum price of bread by decree, thereby causing a rush on the bakeries. To remedy these disorders appeal has to be made to the Governor himself, Don Gonzalo Fernandez de Cordova, who is a very busy man, for he is conducting the siege of Casale in Monferrat, and has no inclination to be bothered with subjects such as bread. Don Gonzalo decrees that the price shall be raised once more; this causes riots, crowds storm the bakeries, and Renzo is surprised to see loaves scattered about the streets.

All Manzoni's crowds behave in absurd and hysterical ways. The crowd lacks the wisdom of the private man in his garden, and the feeling of 'togetherness' undermines reason. Manzoni's view is much the same as Shakespeare's, and we are aware of a close affinity with passages in *Julius Caesar* or *Coriolanus*. ' "Why my lads," the sheriff begins, addressing the crowd, "what are you doing here? Go home. Go home. Where's your fear of God? . . . We don't want to hurt you, but just go off home like good fellows, now. What the devil are you doing here, crowding up like this?" ' But whereas Shakespeare sided with the constituted authorities against the mob, and sympathized with Menenius Agrippa and stood against Jack Cade, for Manzoni laws made by grandees are absurd as well.

Renzo's eye is innocent and shrewd. For him, too, government, starvation, war, are mysterious, they come and go like the seasons. And though his ignorance involves him in the riots, this would not have mattered very much had he not decided to go to an inn for the night. The inn is the *Osteria della Piena Luna*—The Full Moon. It is a typical Lombard inn with solid food, if roughly served on plain tables—there are still many such inns in villages. Worse, Renzo, excited by the strange scenes, gets drunk. The point here is that we do not merely witness the objective antics of a drunken man, we are made to experience the subjective states in a way that is curiously modern. Various issues become confused, as with Joyce or Svevo. There is, of course, the problem of registration at the inn. 'Christian name and surname, nationality and business, whether armed . . .

how long staying in the city.' Renzo has a peasant's caution about signing his name, which is partly based on superstition, but also partly on experience—as often as not when one signs one's name one does in fact part with something, if only money. His refusal to give his name is bellicose—and then, as to be expected, the details are wormed out of him in a moment by an experienced *agent provocateur* or police spy. The grumbling landlord puts Renzo to bed and then, much against his instinct, denounces him to the police. Of course he likes the police no more than another man, but he dares not take the risk of remaining silent. He is, as it were, a kindhearted neutral. If only Renzo had chosen somebody else's inn . . .

The following morning Renzo is arrested by a nervous sheriff's notary and two bailiffs. The notary has to lead his prisoner through streets where the mob is king. Renzo attracts public sympathy, that normal Italian sympathy for a prisoner in the grip of the law. He manages to escape and to flee from Milan, making as fast as he can for the village near Bergamo where his cousin Bartolo lives. At an inn in Gorgonzola he discovers that he has been denounced by the authorities as a major malefactor, and hurries faster on his way. Renzo journeys on foot, with the night breeze stinging his brow, to the gloomy waters of the river Adda, and discovers a Charon to waft him across the river to the territory of the Republic of Venice—'Long live Saint Mark.' And there we leave him, in the company of his cousin and other Lombards who are employed in the silk industry.

Renzo naturally associates with poor people like himself and even the minor rogues that he comes across in his adventures—landlords, notaries or spies—only rob or arrest or spy because they are poor and are afraid. But we now return to the sinister milieu of Don Rodrigo with which Manzoni has no sympathy. Don Rodrigo's plans have been frustrated by Fra Cristofero, but Attilio attempts a revenge. He visits their mutual uncle, who is known as the Conte Zio or Count Uncle and is a member of the Secret Council in Milan. The Conte Zio is a kind of State lawyer, a Quibble-Weaver on the 'Governmental plane', a M. de Norpois.

Ambiguous language, significant silences, sudden pauses in the middle of a sentence, winks that meant 'my lips are sealed', raising hopes without committing himself, conveying a threat amidst elaborate politeness, all were techniques . . . to increase his own importance; so that, eventually, if he said 'I can't do anything

32

about this,' sometimes because it happened to be the absolute truth, he said it in such a way that it was not believed and that, too, served to increase the conception, and hence the reality, of his power—like those boxes still occasionally to be seen in some chemists shops, which have certain words in Arabic on the outside, and nothing inside, but are useful to maintain the prestige of the shop.

The Conte Zio engages in conversations in high quarters, diplomatic conversations of a devious and suggestive kind that are only possible in a high civilisation. After he has had a discussion with the Father Provincial of the Capuchins Fra Cristofero is removed from his convent at Pescarenico, and henceforward Renzo and Lucia have no protector in their district.

Manzoni, like Parini, so disliked the idle rich that his conversations between the 'great' sometimes make us think of Dickens—the difference being that Manzoni belonged to the 'upper classes' and saw their life from within, and could describe a gentleman, such as Cardinal Federigo, whereas Dickens could not; and that Manzoni always wears a velvet glove, his satire is quieter, and words never run away with him. Don Rodrigo, unable to seize Lucia by his own strength, must needs appeal to someone bigger and stronger than himself. The personage to whom he has recourse is quite a big boss and tyrant (in the language that the Fascisti popularised, one would say *Gerarca* or Hierarch) who resides just within the border of Venetian territory and hence can jump from state to state when things become hot. This big boss is so feared that he is never called by name—he is referred to as the *Innominato* or the Unnamed. In the schema of district tyrants whose existence Manzoni with typical irony takes for granted, the Unnamed is an eagle amongst vultures, for 'even foreign princes used his services more than once to carry out some important political assassination'—foreign princes being the most magnificent and rapacious tyrants of all.

Everything about the Innominato, then, is on a bigger scale than Don Rodrigo, and Don Rodrigo is now made to seem a mean and shabby jackal. The Innominato's castle is bigger. It lies 'on top of a bluff jutting from a ragged chain of mountains and joined to them or separated from them—it is difficult to say which—by a mass of crags and precipices, and a labyrinth of caverns and chasms, extending down both sides of it'. Manzoni makes use of natural scenery to reflect a state of mind, rather as Giorgione is said to do with his painting. The descriptions here are a recall to the *Inferno*. The entrance to the Innominato's valley is guarded by a dismal tavern called the Inn of '*Mạlanotte*' or 'Bad Night'. The bravoes of the Innominato are more numerous and more ferocious than those of Don Rodrigo, and they have grotesque names like Dante's devils: *Tarabuso* (Lie-Low), or *Squinternotto* (Screw-Loose). Yet the Innominato has a certain dignity. He approaches Don Rodrigo 'returning his greeting and at the same time looking at his face and hands, as he did from force of habit, almost an involuntary one by now, even with his oldest and most tried friends. He was tall, swarthy and bald; his few remaining hairs were white, and his face was wrinkled, which made him look, at first sight, rather older than his sixty years. But his bearing and movements, the animation of his strongly pronounced features, the sinister but vital flash of his eye, indicated a vigour of body and mind that would have been remarkable in a young man'.

Don Rodrigo has performed services for the Innominato in the past, and accumulated some immoral capital with him; and so, when he asks the Innominato to kidnap Lucia from the convent at Monza, the Innominato agrees as a matter of course.

At this point we come to one of the most hotly disputed sections of the whole book, the conversion of the Innominato. The Innominato is preferable to Don Rodrigo, I have suggested, as a master criminal in a detective story is preferable to a sneak thief. He becomes interested in the kidnapping as soon as Don Rodrigo speaks of its difficulties and dangers. He is in fact something of a pre-Nietzschean hero—or at least this is what Manzoni intends him to be. But he is in a condition of secret crisis owing to a continual struggle between remorse and pride. The crisis comes to a head when Lucia, who has been kidnapped with the connivance of La Signora and Egidio, is brought to the castle by a group of bravoes. The Innominato undergoes a stormy conversion to religion in the space of a night.

I can think of no parallel to the conversion of the Innominato in the work of any other great novelist. Consider how tentatively and by what tangents Dostoevsky approaches the psychology of the religious spirit in *The Idiot* or *The Brothers Karamazov*, or the lengthy process of the still hazy conversion of Pierre Bezuhov in *War and Peace*. The conversion of the Innominato is a sudden objective change from crime and violence to love of God and to Christian charity; and there is no denying that it seems to be a *coup de théâtre* typical of all that is worst in the romantic style.

Manzoni himself, of course, saw things quite otherwise, but the gap between his outlook and that of the average contemporary reader is so wide that one wonders how it is to be bridged, how we are to follow Manzoni into his different world, which we must do if we are to understand him. The conversion of the Innominato can only be explained in terms of a miracle of grace—and this is exactly how one of the simpler characters, a village tailor, does describe it. But then it was precisely in such words that Manzoni explained his own conversion when people asked him about it. We can only understand Manzoni's 'Realism' if we grasp that he believed in the 'real' and 'objective' existence of a supernatural world. Viewed in this light the conversion of the Innominato may well be explained in relation to Lucia's vow to the Madonna that she will sacrifice Renzo if the Madonna will rescue her from her enemies. True, the tension between aggressiveness and badness on the one hand, and humility and charity on the other—whereby the big criminal is potentially the good man on an equally big scale—is rooted in tradition. The conversion of the Innominato resembles the conversion of Fra Cristofero who, before, was quarrelsome and proud but at least not mediocre. Yet for all his technical brilliance, Manzoni is up against a task almost too big for him. Characteristically he tackles it head on and objectively, as distinct from mystically or symbolically; his religion like his vision is Western, 'objective'.

The Innominato in his den is meditating his intention of liberating Lucia.

Who's Don Rodrigo, anyway? Like someone caught by an unexpected and embarrassing question from a superior, the Innominato hastily tried to think of an answer to this query put by himself—or rather by that new self which had grown so alarmingly all of a sudden, and was rising up to judge his former self. Then he began searching round for the reasons which could have led him to assume the task, almost before being asked, of causing so much suffering to a wretched, unknown girl . . . His assent, rather than deliberate, had been the instantaneous reaction of a mind conditioned by his former habits and feelings, a consequence of a thousand former actions. And the tormented self-examiner, so as to account for this one fact, found himself involved in the examination of his whole life. Back, back he went from year to year, from feud to feud, from murder to murder, from crime to crime; each of them came back to his new conscience, isolated from the feelings that had made him want to commit them, so that they reappeared in all the monstrousness which those feelings had prevented him noticing. They were all his, they were him; the horror of this thought, reviving at each fresh memory, clung to them all, and grew at last to desperation. He sat up, frenzied, flung out a frenzied arm to the wall by the bed, snatched a pistol, pulled it down and . . . just at the moment of finishing off a life that had become insupportable, his thoughts, assailed as it were by a posthumous terror and dread, jumped forward into the time which would still be flowing on after his death. With a shudder he pictured his mutilated corpse lying motionless at the mercy of the most abject of survivors . . .

And so on. The psychology, the reconstruction of detail, is a *tour de force*. If Manzoni fails to convince us, this is because, with all his skill, he cannot enfold so great a change within a few pages. But if he fails, at least his failure is magnificent. It is a failure that I can only compare with the failure (it seems to me) of certain passages of Shakespeare; for instance, when Mark Antony, in the lapse of a few minutes, manages to persuade the Romans that the men who killed Caesar are not heroes but murderers. It is better, I think, that such things should happen off-stage. In this Racine is superior to Shakespeare.

The Innominato is a man of spontaneous reactions. He has the habit of making straight for his goal without counting the cost, and he does so now. He determines to call without delay on Cardinal Federigo Borrommeo, the Archbishop of Milan—successor and cousin of the canonized San Carlo—who happens to be making a tour of inspection in the district, surrounded by a throng of priests and devout parishioners. The sudden arrival of the Innominato like a wolf amidst a flock of geese, arouses dismay and terror. The clergy draw back, but the Cardinal receives the Innominato with open arms.

In so far as in both Manzoni interprets the religious and moral soul, the character of Cardinal Federigo recalls that of Fra cristofero. But in all else these heroes of the spirit are unlike, and each has his unique personality. Manzoni describes the Cardinal's background with historical detail, for he is a historical personage. Cardinal Federigo belongs to the great aristocratic family of the Borrommei. He is a man of affluence and learning—he founded the Ambrosian library in Milan. But Manzoni would scarcely have singled him out for praise had he been no more than this. In an age of social anarchy the Cardinal had a highly developed social sense of a practical kind. His was an example of that Northern Italian type of practical morality which leads to the founding of great institutions for the distressed, such as those of Don Bosco or Cottolengo; whereas in the South they tend to concentrate more on the miracles and bi-locations of saints. The Cardinal is essentially an aristocrat, a leader of men, and he is as fearless as the Innominato himself. But if he is charitable, he is also just. 'If there were times when he showed himself severe, even harsh, it was towards those of his subordinate clergy whom he found guilty of avarice or negligence or any other conduct opposed to the spirit of their noble ministry'. We expect that poor Don Abbondio is in for trouble, and we are not mistaken.

The trouble begins immediately. For of course Don Abbondio is to be found amongst the flock of priests who draw back with fright when the Innominato strides through the room. As soon as he hears the Innominato's story the Cardinal summons Don Abbondio, as Lucia's parish priest, and determines to send him to the castle to break the news of her liberation to the girl. Don Abbondio is terrified of the Innominato and terrified of the journey. His reflections while riding his mule to the castle are as undignified as his mulemanship—little reflections on how to have a safe and easy life, and speculations on why so many people are restless or violent. He is an ecclesiastical Sancho Panza.

So Lucia and Agnese are at last brought together again and lodged in the house of a good tailor and his wife, in a peasant house where, nonetheless, 'there was something on the hearth beside the cat'; and we have another of those popular interludes of conversation between the four in which Manzoni is at his happiest. Don Abbondio meanwhile has primed Agnese on what to say to the Cardinal, but when in all simplicity the Cardinal visits the tailor's house to see Lucia, she cannot contain herself, and out the truth comes bubbling:

'If only all priests were like your lordship, taking sides with the poor a bit, instead of getting them into messes so as to save their own skins,' said Agnese . . . annoyed at the thought that Don

Abbondio, after always sacrificing others to his own interests, should expect on top of it to be able to prevent them venting their feelings a little, when there was this rare chance of complaining to someone above them.

'Do say whatever is on your mind,' said the Cardinal.

'I mean that, if our priest had done his duty, things wouldn't have gone this way.'

And so the whole story of Don Rodrigo's threats and of Don Abbondio's cowardice is revealed to the Cardinal. And that only shortly before he is to visit and inspect Don Abbondio's own parish.

But before this situation comes to a head, a more permanent refuge must be found for Lucia. The nearby country seat of some Milanese gentry seems safe enough. The house belongs to an old couple, Don Ferrante and Donna Prassede, who are comic figures of Shakespearean stature. Donna Prassede is what the French call an *araignée de sacristie*, one who is always busy about *oeuvres*, good works, and we expect her overriding interest in life to be the chastity of others. As Manzoni puts it:

> Donna Prassede was an old lady with a strong propensity for doing good—certainly the worthiest profession that man can ply, but one which, like all others, is open to abuse. To do good one must know what it is; and, like everything else, we can only know this by means of our own passions, our own judgments, our own ideas—which often do not amount to very much ... Hence it happened that she would either take as good what was not so in reality, or use means which were apt to have the very opposite effect to her intentions, or think some of these means allowable when they were not so at all, all from a vague presumption that those who go beyond their duty can also go beyond their rights. She often tended either not to see the reality behind facts, or to see realities that were not there at all ...

And so Donna Prassede set about her pious task of reforming Lucia's young mind and of 'bringing back to the right path one who was in sore need of it'. For 'she felt as sure as if she had heard it on good authority that all Lucia's misfortunes were a punishment from heaven for her attachment to that good-for-nothing ... For, as she often told herself and others, her whole object in life was to help carry out the will of heaven, but she often made the great mistake of taking for the will of heaven her own brain . . .'

Perhaps more tiresome characters than Donna Prassede can be found in the annals of Protestant religion. She, at least, is not exactly a hypocrite, nor does she quote unsuitable bits of the Old Testament to drive her points home, and she has never used her influence in public campaigns against pleasure. Yet she is a fair copy-book sketch of a Catholic type. Nearly every town from Calais to Syracuse has its Donna Prassedes, just as it has its Perpetuas.

Don Ferrante, Donna Prassede's husband, is equally comic. He is a 'man of study' and his mind is expressed in his library which we examine like the Priest and the Barber in *Don Quixote*. Don Ferrante is essentially the out-of-date provincial pedant of the kind that flourished in Italy in Manzoni's own time, and indeed may still be found in remoter parts today. He also represents the 'classical' and scholastic type of learning that Manzoni hated. He 'had a considerable collection of books—just under three hundred volumes; all choice works, all by the best reputed authors on various subjects, in each of which he was more or less versed'. We discover, however, that most of his learning was of the dead and useless kind, if not pure charlatanism. 'In astrology he was generally considered, and rightly, to be more than an amateur; for he not only had the generic conceptions and the common vocabulary of the influences, aspects and conjunctions, but he knew how to talk of them aptly and as if *ex cathedra* . . . And for twenty years or so he had upheld the system of Cardano in long and frequent disputes against another learned man who was in fiercely attached to that of Alcabizio . . .'

Don Ferrante

had learned enough philosophy to suffice him, and was continually learning more by reading Diogenes Laertius. But these systems, however fine they may be, cannot all be held at once; and as one must settle on some author if one wants to become a philosopher, Don Ferrante had settled on Aristotle . . . He also had various works by the most learned of his modern disciples; those of his opponents he had always refused either to read (so as not to waste time, he would say) or to buy (so as not to waste money). As an exception, however, he found room in his library for the celebrated twenty-two volume *De Subtilitate*, and for some anti-peripatetic work of Cardano's in consideration of his knowledge of astrology . . .

'Natural history,' we discover, 'he had cultivated more as a recreation than a study', though he had Albertus Magnus' treatise on herbs, plants and animals. But

> Into the secrets of magic and witchcraft he had penetrated rather more deeply, these being sciences . . . much more popular and necessary in those days, and ones in which facts were of much greater importance, and more accessible for verification. . . . But if Don Ferrante could call himself learned in all the above sciences, there was one in which he deserved and enjoyed the title of professor—the science of chivalry. Not only did he argue about it in a most masterly manner, but he was frequently asked to intervene in affairs of honour, and always had some decision to give. In his library, and one might almost say in his head, he had the works of the most renowned writers on this subject—Paride del Pozzo, Fausto da Longiano, Urrea, Muzio, Romei, Albergato, the first and the second *Forno* of Torquato Tasso, all the passages from whose *Gerusalemme Liberata* and *Gerusalemme Conquistata* that could be used as a text on chivalry, he always had at his fingers' ends and could quote from if need be.

This raises another interesting point. Manzoni loathed 'chivalry' as an excuse for idleness and violence, and 'chivalry' was almost an article of faith of the romantic movement.

But we must now return to the poor Don Abbondio who is being asked straight questions by the Cardinal.

' "These saints are peculiar too," Don Abbondio was thinking . . . "Really when one boils it down, he's more concerned about the loves of two young people than about the life of a poor priest." ' Notice that Don Abbondio spontaneously thinks of religion in terms of 'the priest's interest'. 'And for his part he'—Don Abbondio—'would have been only too glad for the conversation to end there; but at every pause he saw the Cardinal waiting and looking as if he expected a reply, a confession or an apology; something anyway. "I can only repeat, Your Grace," he therefore replied, "that I'm in the wrong . . . But courage isn't a thing one can give oneself." '

It is Private Angelo's answer. And the Cardinal's rejoinder, which destroys this wisdom, extends over the chapter. I need scarcely add that what the Cardinal says is totally without effect on Don Abbondio. It goes in at one ear and out at the other. With the Innominato a conversion is possible, but not with Don Abbondio. ' "O what a holy man, but what a worrier," Don Abbondio was thinking. "Even within himself; forever prying and fussing, criticising and cross-questioning; even with himself..." ' And so we leave Don Abbondio, pouring his complaints into the ear of Perpetua and seeking consolation.

At this point the novel moves over once more to the politics of the time. The Governor of Milan, or, to give him his full title, the Captain General of Italy, Don Gonzalo Fernandez de Cordova, has signed a letter denouncing Renzo to the authorities of the Venetian Republic. The Captain General, as we already know, is involved in an affair that has many ramifications. I need not follow Manzoni into them here, save to say that they concern the succession of the Duchy of Mantua, which is of interest to France, Spain, England, the Venetian Signiory, Pope Urban VIII, the House of Savoy and the House of Gonzaga. The focal point of the whole business is still the siege of Casale. Now this siege 'was going badly, dragging on too long, sometimes dragging backwards, owing partly to the steady, wary, resolute conduct of the besieged, partly to his (i.e. Don Gonzalo's) lack of men and partly, if one is to believe the historians, to his many blunders. The latter we will leave an open question, being inclined to find it a very happy circumstance if true, and if because of this a few less men were killed, maimed or lamed in that enterprise, and even, *ceteris paribus*, a few less roof-tiles damaged in Casale.' Nothing is more welcome to rulers in a mess than a scapegoat; and Don Gonzalo welcomes the diversion of denouncing Renzo, whose wickedness has by now become legendary. Manzoni's contemporaries must have been reminded of the denunciations of *carbonari* and liberals by Austrian agents in the early nineteenth century.

Renzo has resort to the classic solution when you are wanted by the authorities—he goes somewhere else and that is that. From his new refuge in the Veneto, with the help of a scribe, he writes to Lucia and receives letters in return from another scribe employed by Agnese. The translation of peasant ideas into literary language by one man, the interpretation by another and the re-translation back into peasant language causes a muddle, especially (we imagine) because these scribes can never put things simply but must add their own baroque ornamentations. Nevertheless Renzo at last grasps some hint of Lucia's vow to the Madonna that she will not marry him, and is in despair. Lucia's situation, languishing under Donna Prassede's interpretation of God's will and Don Ferrante's pedantry, is hardly better. So things drag on until the autumn of the following year.

In the course of the last page or two I have dwelt on many minor details which form the centre of the book, as it were, and link up the two principal parts. I have sometimes been tempted to think that there are really two novels in *I Promessi Sposi*. The first would extend from the crisis with Don Abbondio to the conversion of the Innominato and the liberation of Lucia. When he had reached this point it would have been easy for Manzoni to have dispensed Lucia from her vow—why not through the Cardinal?—and sent her to the Veneto where she and Renzo could marry and settle down (the Cardinal would, of course, have bought Renzo a little silk factory, or at least a cottage). But Manzoni insists that politics should intervene once more. There was no question of anybody settling down that year in the lands along the Po. Had there been any such question we should have missed the occasion for some of the most vivid prose-writing in all Italian literature. For Manzoni, unlike Scott, was not prepared to alter dates so as to simplify the story, or to make cavalier amends to *il vero* in notes at the end of the book.

We return to Milan where public economy, organised and directed by soldiers and noblemen who knew nothing about it, has become chaotic. The muddle can only be compared with what happened in Northern Italy under German-Fascist occupation. There are of course enormous numbers of edicts (a speciality of Italy in times of dictatorship). As Manzoni expresses it: 'If all the edicts at that time had been executed, the duchy of Milan would have had as many citizens on the high seas as England has today.' The people got round the edicts, and the mob and the Government went to more and more absurd lengths. 'The people had tried to create abundance by sacking and burning, the Government was trying to maintain it by the gallows and the rope. Such means were linked to each other, but the reader can see how little they had to do with ends . . .' First came famine. 'All day a confused murmur of voices . . . echoed in the streets; at night there was a chorus of groans, broken every now and then by sudden loud wails, shouts or solemn invocations ending in a piercing scream.' Then followed the plague. But the wars continued, and invading armies drove many inhabitants of the Milanese to seek refuge in the mountains—among them, as we should expect,

Don Abbondio, who was the first to desert his post at the signs of danger, and Perpetua and Agnese. The monotony of Don Abbondio's philosophizing on their journey is broken when the group falls in with a hospitable tailor (the second good tailor), from whom they learn more news of the Innominato's conversion, and how he has turned his castle into a sanctuary for the homeless. Don Abbondio thinks that the castle will be a very suitable place to go to. But to his dismay, when they have reached it, he learns that the Innominato has decided to defend it and the refugees it contains and this means new danger. So they go home again, but when they reach their village at last they find that the houses have been pillaged during their absence, Don Abbondio's buried money has been stolen, and over all there breathes a fetid atmosphere of death.

Manzoni's chapters about the plague have become deservedly famous for the combination of historical method and the selection of vivid detail; and I cannot pretend to give them their due here. They are superior almost beyond compare to the work done on a similar subject by the contemporary French novelist, Albert Camus, in *La Peste*. Manzoni's method, like Camus', consists in building up suspense by the accumulation of significant detail. The plague developed by progressive stages. The first was the stage of anarchy when dread of being conveyed forcibly to the lazar house or 'lazzaretto' prompted people to conceal their symptoms. Then instances 'of death with strange spasms, palpitations, coma, delirium and those fatal symptoms of livid spots and tumours began to grow frequent, first in the quarter round the Porta Orientale, and then in every part of the city.' Soon the lazzaretto swarmed with living corpses, and in this state it was handed over to the administration of the Capuchin order.

The Governor, occupied as usual by trivial rather than essential matters, still sits outside Casale. Terror leads to disorder and anarchy in Milan. Superstitions revive. There is the wild rumour that the plague is being caused deliberately by *untori* or anointers, who plot in secret and spread a deadly poison, an unguent or a powder, in the churches or on the doors of houses. Rewards are offered for the capture of such enemies. People are suspicious of foreigners and strangers. An old man of eighty who is found dusting a bench in church is accused of spreading the plague and carried off to 'prison, judge and torture'. Three young French travellers are arrested for gazing fixedly a the architecture of the Duomo. At this point there is an interesting struggle between the Cardinal and popular feeling. He is absorbed in the practical work of succouring the afflicted, and he prefers tackling the plague this way to exhibiting the relics of his holy predecessor, San Carlo, in which expedient the mob has unlimited confidence. But in the end popular feeling obliges him to give way, and on June 11th the authorities organise a great procession. It so happens that that very same day the death rate has accelerated, and rumours about poisonous powders revive and spread. The population of Milan, which was about a quarter of a million, is reduced to some sixty thousand. The more it extends the more macabre the plague becomes. There are processions of death carts; and plague commissioners and servants known as *monatti*, or *apparitori*, swollen in numbers, wield dictatorial powers. Absurd scientific and astrological theories spread with the crime and panic. Don Ferrante denies the existence of the plague with learned arguments. ' "*In rerum natura*," he would say, "there are only two kinds of things; substances and accidents; and if I prove that the contagion cannot be one or the other, I shall have proved that it does not exist, that it is a chimera. And here we go . . ." *His fretus*—that is to say on these excellent grounds—he took no precaution against the plague, caught it, and went to bed to die, like a hero of Metastasio, blaming the stars.'

Manzoni was so interested in the historical aspects of the plague that for once he was in danger of being carried off his point. Fortunately he decided to publish much of what he wrote on this subject in a separate work: *Storia della Colonna Infame*, which he first printed in 1840 as an appendix to the revised version of the novel. We are thus able to turn to the principal characters of the fiction and learn of the effect of the plague on them.

This effect is conveyed by a series of clear details of the highest dramatic quality. The first sufferer we meet is Don Rodrigo.

One night towards the end of August . . . Don Rodrigo was on his way home, in Milan, accompanied by the faithful Griso, one of the three or four who had remained alive out of his whole household . . . That day Don Rodrigo had been one of the merriest; and, among other things, had made the whole company laugh by a sort of funeral oration on Count Attilio who had been carried off by the plague two days before . . . As he walked along, however, he felt a sort of uneasiness, a heaviness, a weakness of the legs . . .

Manzoni disposes of Count Attilio, as of a trivial person whom nobody cares about; one of those people about whom, when we say to a friend: 'Did you know so-and-so is dead?' we are answered only by an 'Oh, *is* he?' Notice how Don Rodrigo's social set dies as pointlessly as it lived. The crisis develops. Don Rodrigo is a coward and he knows perfectly well what his servant, Griso, is thinking. The page devoted to his fever and nightmare of disintegration corresponds to the creative nightmare of the Innominato when in the throes of conversion. When he awakes Don Rodrigo knows that his only hope lies in avoiding the *monatti* who will carry him away to the lazzaretto. He instructs Griso to fetch a doctor who can be bribed to keep silence. Soon after Griso's departure he hears the sinister tinkling of the bells that the *monatti* wear over their shoulders to announce their presence; and with them is Griso who has betrayed him. He is carried off by the *monatti* as a soul in Dante's hell is carried off by devils. But Griso's own fate is no better than his master's.

Griso stayed behind, choosing hurriedly whatever was most useful to him. He made a bundle of the lot and went off. He had carefully avoided touching the *monatti* or letting himself be touched by them. But in that last frenzied search he had taken his master's clothes up from the bedside and shaken them to see if there was any money in them, without thinking of anything else. He was forced to think about it, however, next day, when as he was carousing in a tavern, his strength failed him and he collapsed. Abandoned by his companions he fell into the hands of the *monatti* who despoiled him of whatever he had on him worth having and threw him on a cart, on which he died before reaching the lazzaretto where his master had been taken.

At long last we return to Renzo who is still in the Veneto. The plague had crossed the frontier and Renzo had contracted it and recovered. He is thus immune; he belongs to the aristocracy of plague-time. By now, of course, formal regulations have broken down and, mastered by his longing for home, Renzo returns to his native village.

There is something, I feel, about Renzo's longing for home, for the poetry of the smoke rising from his own hearth, that we must compare to Ulysses' nostalgia for Ithaca. Critics have noticed that

Manzoni never treats of *amore*, or love, in *I Promessi Sposi*—that subject which is overstressed and hackneyed in Italian life as in opera, whose librettos are often an elaborate superstructure on the fact that *amore* rhymes with *cuore* (heart).[1] And *I Promessi Sposi* is no more a 'love story' than the *Odyssey*. It is a marriage story, the story of the foundation of a household, a home, and that includes a whole life of attachments—to one's mountains and plains, to one's children, to one's friends and to one's epoch of history.

But when Renzo returns to his village, he finds that it has become a waste. The first person upon whom his eyes fall is, symbolically, the village idiot; and then he sees Don Abbondio who, hardly inspiring at the best of times, is certainly not on this occasion for he cannot disguise his discontent and his fear that Renzo may bring trouble with him. But Renzo's sense of ruin is completed only when he sees his vineyard. We all have different ways of measuring wealth. In the City of London they still measure it by shares in Indo-Chinese rubber or Ceylon tea, but for the Italian countryman property is not an abstraction in a bank; it is a house, a garden, a field that you can see. Renzo's garden is a desolation—worse, it is a blasphemy.

> There was a riot of nettles, ferns, tares, dog-grass, coltsfoot, wild oats, amarinth, dandelion, sorrel, foxgloves and other plants of the kind . . . There was a medley of stems, each trying to grow higher in the air than the other, or crawl past each other on the ground and get the best place at any cost; a jumble of leaves, flowers, fruits, of a hundred different colours, shapes and sizes; ears of barley and Indian corn, tufts and bunches and clusters with little heads of white and red, yellow and blue.

Manzoni's accumulated description of creeping disorder reinforces his descriptions of the plague, and prepares us for worse to come. Poor Renzo; the waste of good land is a kind of blasphemy or sin to him, like the ruin of a canvas to an artist. So he sets out, through Monza and Greco for Milan, to seek out Agnese; directing his steps

[1] One critic, Umberto Calosso, in his *Colloqui con Manzoni*, has gone so far as to suggest that Renzo did much better to get drunk in the Osteria della Piena Luna than to *fare all'amore* or to spend all his time in a condition of sex obsession like many young Italians. In the lives of Italian men and women *l'amore* is rather like drunkenness in the lives of the English or Americans.

by the distant cathedral which looks like a white ship upturned when seen from the slight undulations to the north of the city.

Renzo's second experience of Milan is not one of confusion and absurdity, but of horror. The city has now become a hell, and can only be described by borrowing from Dante. The orchestration of the opening passage is a warning:

'The weather was close, the air heavy, the sky veiled all over by an even cloud, or rather haze, which seemed to blot out the sun without giving any promise of rain. The countryside around was partly uncultivated, and entirely parched. All the vegetation looked discoloured and there was not even a drop of dew on the withered, drooping leaves. This solitude, this silence so near a great city added a new disturbance to Renzo's disquiet and made his thoughts gloomier than ever.' Renzo manages to get past the infernal walls (one thinks of the city of Dis) by offering a bribe (the bribe to Cerberus) at the Porta Nuova. He walks along by the gloomy Naviglio canal. But his dilemma is still Dante's and Virgil's. How is he to ask the way? The first man he accosts wards him off with a stick for he fears Renzo is an 'anointer'. And then, in the desolation of this hell, Renzo begins to discover signs of devils and lost souls.

At every step he took, certain noises which he had first heard as he stood there talking were growing louder and louder; the rumble of wheels and the clatter of horses, with a tinkle of little bells, and every now and again the crack of whips, to the accompaniment of curses. He looked ahead of him but saw nothing. On reaching the end of the street and coming into the square of San Marco, the first things to meet his eye were two upright beams with a rope and various pulleys; and he did not take long to recognize an object familiar enough in those days, the abominable instrument of torture . . . It was one of those extreme and ineffectual remedies which at that time . . . were used very prodigally.

Renzo's next vision is of an *apparitore* leading some carts heaped with corpses that are surmounted by *monatti*. Other *monatti* are raiding a quarter of the city seeking out their prey. In the midst of these scenes of horror there are occasional acts of heroism or love—hell has its Paolo and Francesca. A mother delivers her dead child to the *monatti* and by her dignity and with a bribe, instils them with a momentary respect: and then, as though speaking over her shoulder, says: 'When you pass this way tonight, come up and fetch me too, and not me alone'—for she has yet another dying child with her, and she herself is certain to die. But more often there is no dignity to redeem the squalour of these scenes in Manzoni's *Inferno*.

Unfortunately the mob takes Renzo for an anointer, and tries to kill him (another crowd!). He can only escape by leaping upon a passing death cart. The *monatti* take his side against the mob. One of them shouts to Renzo: ' "Leave them to me"; and tearing a filthy rag off one of the bodies, he quickly tied it into a knot, took it by one of the ends, raised it towards the stubborn group like a sling and made as if to throw it, shouting: "Just you wait, you rabble." At these gestures they all fled in terror, and Renzo saw nothing but enemies' backs and heels glancing in the air like hammers in a clothing mill.'

The *monatti*, like the devils in the *Inferno*, become more macabre as they become more comic. When Renzo thanks one of them for saving his life: ' "Don't mention it," said the *monatto*, " . . . You're quite right to anoint those swine; anoint away and exterminate all these people, who aren't worth a thing until they're dead . . ." "Long live the plague, and death to the rabble," exclaimed the other; and with this fine toast he put the flask to his mouth, and holding it there with both hands against the jolting of the cart, then offered it to Renzo, saying: "Drink to our health." '

Accompanied by drunken singing on the death cart, Renzo at last reaches the lazzaretto. This is the deepest circle of hell. There was a loud and continuous singing of *villanelle*.

The very air and sky increased . . . the horror of all around him. The mist had gradually thickened and woven into big clouds, which, as they grew darker, would have looked like warnings of a stormy night, had there not appeared in the very midst of that glum and lowering sky and as if through a thick veil, the pale disk of the sun, diffusing a dim, feeble light but pouring out a heavy suffocating heat. Every now and again, amidst the continual buzzing of that confused multitude could be heard a rumble of thunder, deep, jerky, as if irresolute . . .

In the heart of the lazzaretto Renzo falls in with Fra Cristofero, who is devoting the remainder of his time on earth to relieving the sick. The friar accompanies Renzo to the pallet of Don Rodrigo, who is now a cowering wretch, and Renzo is obliged to forgive him. It is in the lazzaretto that the hero discovers Lucia who, like himself, had contracted the plague and has recovered from it. From Lucia he hears the full story of the vow to the Madonna. She is dispensed from it by Fra Cristofero. As Renzo leaves the lazzaretto the rain begins to fall in big heavy drops, a prelude to the torrential downpour that in the end washed away the plague; this Manzoni employs as a symbol of renewal and fresh life and, I think, Divine Grace.

There now remain only a few ends to disentangle. Don Rodrigo is dead and Don Abbondio has nothing more to fear—he can settle down again to his old egotistical life. 'Parish priests,' he says 'are the ones who pull the cart along.' He banters with Renzo good-humouredly. The couple have a pedestrian marriage in the village church and leave for their adopted country near Bergamo.

Thus the tone on which the novel ends is neither classical nor yet romantic in the common meaning of the words. The novel ends in a marriage, yet the marriage is not the end. Renzo and Lucia fade out, as it were; they merge their lives with those of innumerable other working people, with the landscapes, the little factories, the bad politicians and all the rest. They change as ordinary people change with marriage; they become more ordinary. Lucia no longer blushes, her tongue is sharper and more confident; Renzo has his sombre moods.

And she [i.e. Lucia] once found herself asking her moralist, 'what do you think I have learnt? I never went looking for troubles; they came looking for me . . . Unless you mean to say,' she added, smiling sweetly, 'that my mistake was to love you and to promise myself to you.'

Renzo at first found himself in rather a difficulty. After discussing the question and casting together a long time for a solution, they came to the conclusion that troubles often come to those who bring them on themselves, but that not even the most cautious and innocent behaviour can ward them off; and that, when they come—whether by our own fault or not—confidence in God can lighten them and turn them to our own improvement. This conclusion though it was reached by poor people has seemed so just to us that we have thought of putting it down here as the gist of the whole tale.

IV

The Place of 'I Promessi Sposi' in Literature

I have given a long account of Manzoni's novel because it is very little known. I am fully aware that I have not done it justice. To begin with it does not translate easily, and however able the translation, much of the peculiar virtue of the idiom is lost. Moreover an abridged account, such as I have provided, inevitably leaves an impression of looseness of form, of imprecision, and of the stale paraphernalia of the early nineteenth century.

The *Promessi Sposi* is accepted almost unanimously by Italian critics as the greatest novel in Italian literature, and it occupies a place more important than that in Italian life. It is not a book that interests only an *élite* of readers; it is essentially a *popular* book. People who otherwise read very little know the story of Renzo and Lucia almost by heart as they know the librettos of Verdi's operas. Characters such as Don Abbondio and Perpetua and the Conte Zio have become proverbial in the language—they are a part of Italian life as Don Quixote and Sancho are a part of Spanish life. Italians see in *I Promessi Sposi* a mirror of their national character. To know Italy we must appreciate Manzoni, but to appreciate Manzoni, I sometimes feel, we must know Italy; and I am not sure of the way out of this vicious circle.

Manzoni's novel was written well over a century ago. Few foreign critics appreciated it in the nineteenth century; though those who did, Goethe and Edgar Allan Poe, were among the most discerning men of their age. Over a century passed before a complete translation was available in English. There still remains the difficulty of placing the novel in our categories of ideas about literature; it is unlike anything else, in ideology, outlook and treatment. Though written in the early nineteenth century it belongs to that age only superficially. It is unlike *War and Peace*, unlike Scott and Dickens, unlike Balzac or Flaubert, though it bears some surface resemblances to each. Must we then judge the novel in terms of Cervantes? This, certainly, would be no more mistaken. It is a most unusual phenomenon for a novel to be born outside its (European) time: yet *I Promessi Sposi* is an example of exactly that. In consequence, at least abroad, the novel was buried under a heap of misunderstandings.

Certain things, obviously, contributed to the misunderstanding.

Manzoni belonged to no category yet he was naturally judged in terms of the categories that prevailed. He wrote a historical novel which was originally suggested to him by Scott's historical novels, and at a time when Scott was the fashion all over Europe it was naturally supposed that he was an imitator of Scott. And the comparison was made in every way to Manzoni's disadvantage. For whereas Scott turned out his historical novels at the rate of one or two a year, his imitator, with great labour, as it appeared, had only managed to produce one novel. Moreover he presented the public with the picture of an Italy that did not interest it. The European public wanted to know about the melancholy and romantic Italy, a land of golden ruins and squalour and passion, the Italy that Byron had taught it to love, the Italy that Madame de Staël painted in *Corinne* or that Lamartine wept about in *Graziella*. Renzo, with his pedestrian ambitions, is the very antithesis of a romantic figure. He was too common, too plebeian to be interesting. We are only just recovering to-day from the inheritance of the romantic vision of Italy—thanks partly to the very unromantic experience that hundreds of thousands of common soldiers had of that country during the war, partly to the new Italian novel and the new Italian cinema. Manzoni's novel is only understandable if we can view Italians as ordinary people whose problems are very similar to those of other ordinary people in other countries, if we can imagine Italy without the mandoline.

If I repeatedly refer to Stendhal's *Chartreuse de Parme* in the course of this little book, it is because the *Chartreuse* is the only novel about Italy that has the same stature as the *Promessi Sposi*. Indeed in a way these two novels, because so opposite, are complementary; they present two facets of the country as it really is and are essential reading for anyone who wants to understand the Italian character. The Italy that fascinated Stendhal was the Italy of the salons and of high political life, of Machiavellian intrigue and of *amour passion*. Stendhal's Italy still exists. The Sanseverina is still to be met with in Roman salons, and Count Mosca re-lived amongst the kinder and lazier Fascist Gerarchi, who pottered in Roman bureaus and paid lip-service all round and made illicit fortunes between the two wars. And therefore it is scarcely surprising to find out that Stendhal thought very little of *I Promessi Sposi*. He inhibited the poor, pedestrian Italy, and needed to do so for the sake of his art. Manzoni, less brilliant, was more realist.

Perhaps the most telling misunderstanding arose about the relations between Manzoni and Scott. In England and America today Scott is thoroughly out of fashion. But if he is overestimated by schoolmasters, he is underestimated by many critics. Though he was a founder of the romantic novel, he was a far better craftsman—at least in his Scottish novels—than many of the writers who came after him. He could never have been guilty of writing books that were merely grotesque, such as Victor Hugo's *Han d'Islande* or *L'Homme qui rit*. Yet it is not illuminating to compare Manzoni with Scott because Manzoni was not interested in romantic situations as such; he moulded his work quite differently around the skeleton of a similar plot, and he was a writer of much greater stature.

I want to emphasize this last point because in the back of our minds we may have a sneaking feeling that Italians exaggerate the importance of Manzoni because they have so few great novels and because Manzoni wrote only one book. Now if we examine Scott's novels carefully we find that the range of his study of human character is really very limited. Certain types occur in novel after novel under a new disguise. There is the type of ranting Scottish Covenanter who is always quoting the Bible—once Scott begins writing ranting dialogue it is as though he is unable to stop, as though he has found a good parlour trick that amuses his English readers; there is the type of man who performs huge exploits of alcoholic athleticism and drinks himself under the table; and so on. Moreover Scott was a diffuse writer.

Manzoni is misleading. When we first glance at his pages he *appears* diffuse. But examine closely and you will find that he is the tersest of writers, that nearly every word has been closely examined and has its point, that he sketches in more, and more varied, characters in his one novel than are to be found in the whole of Scott.

In this respect I think we would be nearer the mark if we compared Manzoni with Shakespeare. Manzoni knew no English and could only read Shakespeare in translation. Yet internal evidence seems to show that Manzoni had Shakespeare very much in mind when he was writing *I Promessi Sposi*. Manzoni's personages are individuals, not types, and individuals on an almost Shakespearean scale. We know them as we know Shallow and Simple, Bardolph or those people who appear for one moment in a crowd and then are gone for ever. I think of the landlord of the Full Moon Inn and his wife; the notary who arrested Renzo in Milan; the landlord at Renzo's village; the landlord of the inn at Gorgonzola; the boy of twelve called Menico in Renzo's village; the cousins Gervasio and Tonio; the man who foamed at the mouth in the riots at Milan and kept a ragged handkerchief to his blood-stained hair; the Commissioner Ferrer. We never learn the names of many of the characters; they are just people, each with his own special life, like the people we watch in a bus or talk with for five minutes in a bar. Boccaccio had an even wider vision than Manzoni; the *Decameron* is crammed with these bright little sketches in colour. But for terseness and concentration Manzoni is second only to Boccaccio.

A second important influence over Manzoni, of course, was Goethe, indisputably the greatest writer of the epoch. There are traces of the *Sturm und Drang* Goethe, the Goethe of *Götz von Berlichingen* and *Egmont* in Manzoni's lyrical tragedies, and in some scenes of passion in *I Promessi Sposi*. But the later Apollonean Goethe must not be forgotten either. Manzoni's natural descriptions seem to me to retain something of that classical or neo-classical stylisation that was in the air of his age, the stylisation of natural descriptions in the *Iphigenie* or in the *Wahlverwandschaften*, the stylisation of the Empire painters.

I do not want to stress this point too much because my impression may be personal, and nothing is easier than reading something of one's own likings into books one admires. But there is no doubt in my mind that in his comparative solitude and isolation Manzoni spent much more time meditating on the major masterpieces of European literature than on the more transient writing of his time, and it is this that gives his work its disconcerting timelessness.

Another constituent, as I have already made sufficiently plain, was the *Divine Comedy*. But nearer still to Manzoni, both in style and in spirit, I think, is Virgil. Some of Manzoni's descriptions of landscapes have been called 'decadent'. But if they are, they are so with the decadence of Virgil's *Eclogues*:

> Et jam summa procul villarum fulmina fumant
> maioresque cadunt altis de montibus umbrae.

Dr Umberto Calosso, in his *Colloqui col Manzoni*, has found a passage in *I Promessi Sposi* which, he thinks, exactly represents this selfsame experience of eventide in the north Italian village some eighteen hundred years later: 'There was that murmur of bees that we hear in a village upon the evening which, shortly after, gives way to the quiet solemnity of night ... When the doors were opened, here and there were to be seen the fires lighted for the supper of the poor ...' But I believe I could find such parallels and half-memories dating from Manzoni's lonely studies in Somaschi and Barnabiti colleges, when I re-read the description of the lake of Como under the moonlight:

> There was not a breath of wind; the lake lay flat and smooth, and would have seemed quite motionless save for the gentle, tremulous swaying of the moon, reflected from high up in the sky. The only sounds were the slow sluggish lapping of the waves on the pebbly shore, farther away the gurgle of water swishing round the piles of the bridge, and then the measured splash of those two oars, as they cut the surface of the lake, suddenly came out dripping and then plunged in once more ...

Here, there is I think, more than an echo of the description of the sea and the moon and night in the *Aeneid*:

> Iamque fere mediam caeli nox humida metam
> contigerat; placida laxarant membra quiete
> sub remis fusi per dura sedilia nautae ...

Virgil's influence seems to me as evident in Manzoni's outlook as on his style. He has an *anima naturaliter Christiana* and much the same sort of *pietas* and sense of loyalty to the *foyer*, to the pledged word, the same stress on the virtues of patience, simplicity and frugality. He had the same dislike of violence, and even his outlook on nature, I consider, owes at least as much to the *Georgics* as to the writers who were his contemporaries. And this gives the reader of Manzoni a feeling of fundamental serenity which is so rare in modern literature that one suspects it is 'provincial' or 'parochial'.

Manzoni's influence abroad remained at a standstill during the nineteenth century, but in Italy it went on increasing, and it became more and more widely recognized that his novel held up a mirror to his fellow countrymen in which they could see reflected both their virtues and their defects. He had many imitators. One of the first was his son-in-law Massimo D'Azeglio who tried with two novels, *Ettore Fieramosca* and *Niccolo de' Lapi*, to arouse the pride of Italians by depicting the courage and devotion of their ancestors. These novels are still read in Italy, but their weaknesses only show up Manzoni's strength; they are little better than thrillers written on historical subjects. Niccolo Tommaseo also tried his hand at the historical novel in *Il Duca di Atene*. He was a better writer, perhaps, than D'Azeglio; but he lacked width of vision and tried to make up for his defects by preciosity of style.

Indeed it is significant that Manzoni's most fertile influence was not in the disputable field of the historical novel; and this goes to show that the *historical* aspect of Manzoni's work was really only secondary. In the nineteenth century, in literature as in politics, Italy oscillated between realism and rhetoric, and all Manzoni's influence was on the side of the first. Two outstanding poets, Leopardi and Giosue Carducci, escaped from the current of Manzoni's influence for special reasons. Carducci, in the second half of the century, went back to some of the sources of inspiration that Manzoni had denounced, and founded some of his best verse on the pagan and classical sensibility of Horace. Neo-paganism reached its high tide with the rhetoric of D'Annunzio, only to die away in the arid sands of the Fascist movement.

It is not easy to present a picture of Italian literature in terms of schools and influences because Italy tends to produce peculiar giants —the last example was Benedetto Croce—who escape from them by the power of their individuality. The Italian novelist of the eighties, Antonio Fogazzaro, was obviously indebted to Manzoni, and he shared Manzoni's religious faith. But even here we find a marked difference, for Fogazzaro saw faith in terms of extreme tensions between passion and spiritual vocation, and lacked Manzoni's Virgilian sense of faith as reverence and *pietas* by nature linked up with the seasonal round of labour.

Probably Manzoni's most lasting effect should be sought among the new realist novelists, who began with the Sicilian Giovanni Verga and have continued down to our own time and have many representatives among the younger generation of Italian writers today. At first sight it may seem merely paradoxical to say that a novelist such as Alberto Moravia, who dwells on the *bas-fonds* of social life and of sexual experience, owes anything to Manzoni. But it only remains paradoxical if we insist on seeing Manzoni as a pious old romantic, which is not at all the way Italians see him. For Manzoni taught Italians how to reflect character and detail with truth;

he forged the language that modern novelists use and in this sense he is their father, as they themselves are the first to admit.[1]

V

Controversial Points

(i) Manzoni's Religion

As I have already pointed out, Manzoni's attitude to religion has been criticized both by clericals and by anti-clericals. Some critics are unable to see how Manzoni managed to conciliate his lifelong devotion to the Catholic Church with his political opinions, and have therefore suggested that his Catholicism was unorthodox or his liberalism superficial. I believe these views are based on a misunderstanding.

Manzoni's main piece of writing on a controversial religious subject was his *Osservazioni sulla Morale Cattolica* (*Observations on Catholic Ethics*) which he published in 1819. It appeared at a time when he had been successively under the influence of two Jansenist priests, Degola and Tosi, and it consists of answers to accusations against the Catholic Church in Italy made by the Swiss Protestant, Sismondi, in his history of the Italian Republics. The substance of Sismondi's argument is too well known to require emphasis here. Catholic morality, he maintained, which involves practises such as the confessional, and beliefs such as that in indulgences, had corrupted the Italian character and made it weak and dishonest. Manzoni defends both Catholic practises and the Italian character. If Italians are morally corrupt, this is because they fail to live up to Catholic morality. Moreover it is easy to exaggerate, and the Italians as a people have many noble virtues. Manzoni goes on to answer most of the other criticisms that were current amongst Protestants in the nineteenth century. This work has been compared with Newman's *Apologia*. But as it is neither passionate nor personal, it tends to be rather boring. It is written in the muted, deliberately pedestrian style of all Manzoni's essays. The author's politeness and calm are certainly not what we

---

[1] Alberto Moravia once told me that among the Italian writers who most impressed him were Boccaccio, Manzoni and Verga.

expect from an inter-denominational controversy of that period. There are no mystical flights. Granting the premise of faith, his appeal is to reasonableness and common sense. His primary emphasis is on the moral and social aspects of religion. He never had an over-riding interest in the more superficial practises of Italian piety, and he was more concerned about God than about any calendar of minor saints or collection of blessed objects.

At the time of his conversion, and in the years that followed, Manzoni was influenced by Jansenist priests, and he never lost his admiration for Pascal. It is also possible that he felt the spell of his first wife who, though she became a Catholic, was by birth a Swiss Calvinist—and he who says 'Swiss Calvinist' in Italy implies rigid if not Puritan morals. Some Italian critics have laboured long to enumerate traces of Jansenism in Manzoni's works. They have noted, for instance, that there is no mention of the Jesuits in *I Promessi Sposi*, though that order was very powerful in Milan in the early seventeenth century. However this may be they tend, I suspect, to over-emphasize the grip of the Jansenist spirit over Manzoni. No-one denies that Jansenism has had a lasting influence over Catholicism in France. But the movement was foreign to the Italian traditions and temperament, and it never took root beyond the Alps.

I would like to develop this point a little. We associate the Jansenist spirit in France with an excessive rigorism about morals, an excessive preoccupation with sin, a gloomy view of man's guilt, or the establishment of a kind of antithesis between this world and the Divine Kingdom, between the flesh and the spirit. The influence of this tradition is as plain in those who have reacted against it, such as M. Henri de Montherlant, as in those who have in some measure embraced it such as M. François Mauriac.[1] Now plenty of Italian writers have had rigorous morals, but I cannot think of a single one whose work has been inspired by Jansenism in this sense. Indeed *I Promessi Sposi* seems to me a most un-Jansenistic book. There is no bitter strife between this world and the supernatural in Manzoni, or between pleasure and the good. I think that his basic and inherited Italian humanism was too strong for any such feelings to cloud his

[1] Numbers of people have noticed something similar in the novels of Graham Greene. But the English 'sense of sin' does not have a Jansenist origin; presumably it stems out of Calvinism. It would be worth while comparing Tolstoy with Manzoni also. Tolstoy was a Puritan; Manzoni was not.

work. If the religion of the *Promessi Sposi* has a fault, this lies in the sentimental and facile piety which is typically Italian, as I have already pointed out.

Certainly Manzoni had severer ideas about ethics and social obligations than are commonly to be found in Italy. The Jansenist influence probably had something to do with this. But so had Italian writers such as Parini and Rosmini, and the increased sense of responsibility that was in the air of the age. Not only did Manzoni derive from a religious tradition that was already flourishing in Northern Italy, he contributed to it and helped to extend it.

Catholicism is one faith, yet its tone varies from country to country according to the history and psychology of the peoples. The Catholicism of Lombardy or Venetia is sensibly different from that of France, or Spain, or Naples. At a time when other countries were feudal, and then developed absolute monarchies out of their feudalism, the traditions of Lombardy and the Veneto were republican and commercial. The enemies of the Milanese were the absolute monarchs of Spain and Austria.

This explains a good deal of what happened at the time of the Restoration in Italy. For the ideology of the Restoration, as expressed by writers like Bonald and Joseph de Maistre, who more or less identified the claims of absolute monarchy with those of the Church, could not have the same appeal in Italy as in France or Spain. It did not seem unnatural to Manzoni to associate his Catholicism with liberalism, because the liberals seemed to represent the cause of Christianity against proud and powerful oppressors. This view—the identification of the Christian cause with the cause of the poor oppressed Italians—was one of the *leitmotifs* of the Risorgimento. Silvio Pellico, the author of *I miei Prigioni*, was one amongst many who propagated it. There is still a strong Catholic liberal movement in the Veneto and Lombardy to-day. Manzoni's influence helped to foster that tolerant spirit in Italian Catholicism which eventually found its expression in the Christian parliamentary parties which have been the strongest single force opposing the Machiavellian and D'Annunzian tradition in Italian politics.

One final point: though profoundly religious, Manzoni was at no time a 'clerical'. This emerges from all his writings. And in old age he made it once again clear when he accepted the honorary citizenship of Rome shortly after the city had been annexed to the Kingdom of Italy. In his attitude to purely 'clerical' questions, such as the temporal power of the Papacy, he maintained an independent view which is as old as the *Divina Commedia*.

(ii) The Problem of Language

Stendhal made some acute observations about the Italian language in *Rome, Naples et Florence en 1817* (entry of April 10th):

> In the twelfth century various Italian regions—Venice, Florence, Rome, Naples, Milan and Piedmont—spoke different languages. Naturally the region that enjoyed freedom had the finest ideas and its language triumphed. But, most unfortunately, this language never completely subjugated its rivals and so today the literary Italian language is only spoken in Florence and Rome; in all other cities the ancieht dialect is still employed, and one makes oneself ridiculous if one speaks *Tuscan* in conversation.
>
> Anyone writing a letter begins by opening a dictionary and then no expression is too pompous or powerful for him. That explains why terseness, simplicity and the *nuances* of natural style are unknown in Italy.
>
> Anyone who has such gifts writes in Milanese or Venetian. Tuscan is always spoken to foreigners, but when the speaker needs to express a vigorous idea he invariably has recourse to the expressions of his dialect. An Italian writer dedicates three quarters of his studies to the mechanism of language; his constant preoccupation is to avoid words that are not to be found in authors quoted by the Crusca.

Stendhal was writing at a period when the Italian language was going through one of its periodical crises, and he added a number of common-sense criticisms. He pointed out that the worst excesses of pedantry were found among Florentine men of letters; that Italian lacked clear ideas, that it cannot express ideas in a hurry, that it is not a vehicle for comedy and so on. There is plenty of wit in Italy, but it is confined to the dialects. What Stendhal said was of course exaggerated, and it is not accurate to say that the literary language was identical with any spoken language, but nonetheless he gives a vivid picture of the situation.

By 1817 the debate had become acrimonious. There were various schools of thought on the subject. Some writers favoured the *lingua letteraria* as such (the language, that is, of the Academy of the Crusca), others maintained that this was a dead language and that real living Italian was the daily speech of educated Florentines. Manzoni, like Dante and like Machiavelli, made his contributions to the literature on this subject. These included a treatise which he never completed, a letter *Sulla lingua Italiana* addressed to Giacinto Carena, a piece *Dell' unità della lingua e dei mezzi di diffonderla*, two letters to Ruggero Bonghi (1868), and an *Appendice alla Redazione* (1869).

I have already mentioned some of the difficulties Manzoni had to overcome. The familiar language of his household was not Tuscan but *meneghin* (the dialect of Milan). *Meneghin* has a literature: one of Manzoni's near contemporaries, Carlo Porta, had written vivid satirical pieces in it. But one difficulty about *meneghin* is that it is not well understood outside Lombardy. Manzoni could have thrown in the sponge and written in French—he would not have been the first Italian to do this—but this would hardly have fitted in with his patriotism or his feeling as an artist for Italian prose.

So a third solution had to be found. Manzoni sided with those who maintained that the literary language was incapable of conveying ideas and images in an exact and living way. It was impossible to write in a living way without writing in a spoken language, that is, a dialect—and of dialects Florentine was by far the most developed and varied. But Manzoni did not solve his problem merely by reaching this conclusion. He had still to perfect his knowledge of Florentine. To do this he spent some time in Florence and, back in Milan, he was always questioning Florentine friends about the exact meaning of phrases. Even so his efforts were not crowned with complete success. He re-wrote his novel, purging it of French and Lombard idioms; but on some points of detail either his informers or his ear deceived him, and men of learning ever since have been able to enjoy pointing out all his mistakes. Nevertheless the language he did develop became the language of modern Italian prose and has been used ever since.

That Manzoni, who liked ordinary common people and 'romanticism' or realism, should have preferred a living language to the dead stylised language of the 'classicists' and Arcadians was to be expected. But his decision still left peculiar problems. For better or worse he was debarred from one of the common resources of the novelist —the use of local dialect to drive home a feeling of place (like Scott's Scots or Dickens' Cockney). Perpetua, Renzo, Lucia and the others have to talk Tuscan, and this has non-Lombardic local associations. Since Manzoni's time, especially through the radio and newspapers, Italian has become more or less standardised, though the dialects are still spoken at home amongst the poor. Manzoni's way of overcoming this difficulty in his dialogue seems to me brilliant.[1]

The style of I Promessi Sposi is complicated. In fact Manzoni threads together several distinct styles. There is the ironical style; there is the deliberately muted and pedestrian style; and there is yet a third style when he is describing natural scenery or emotions—a famous example is Lucia's farewell to her native hills, and her thoughts in a boat on the moonlit lake of Como. These last poetic passages were added or at least embellished in the later editions of the novel.

(iii) Romanticism

'In Milan,' wrote Manzoni in a famous letter of 1833 in which he expressed his ideas on the romantic movement, 'where it has been more often discussed and at greater length than elsewhere, the word romanticism, unless I am mistaken, has been used to describe a set of ideas that is more reasonable, ordered and general than in any other city.' What in fact did Manzoni mean by romanticism? In what sense can we agree with him when he claims that he himself is a romantic?

The answer to the first question is easy. By 'classicism' Manzoni meant Arcadianism, the servile imitation of the classics, the extravagant use of classical mythology and 'rules based on special facts and not on general principles, on the authority of rhetoricians and not on reasoning—especially that of the authorities in drama'. By 'romanti-

---

[1] It is very difficult for a non-Italian to judge subtle questions of language. Italian appears very simple on the surface, but it is really very complicated and has innumerable *nuances*. But to give a very rough idea of how I think Manzoni succeeded I would remind the reader of those novels by Graham Greene that are about life in London suburbs. Greene does not convey Cockney by silly spelling, substituting 'piper' for 'paper' and so on. He does it by using Cockney syntax. By this means he is able to do something even more difficult than conveying pure Cockney; he manages to manipulate the dreary and tired suburban language which is not Cockney nor yet classical English. We hear the 'off-accent' of his suburban girls. Allowing for all the differences, it was in a comparable way that Manzoni conveyed the mentality and language of Italian common people.

cism' Manzoni understood a reaction against all this, though his reaction was essentially reasonable and measured. He disliked extravagant romanticism for the same reasons as he disliked classicism, he disliked the 'witches, spectres, systematic disorder, the search for extravagance, in so many words the abandonment of common sense' as much as he disliked the loves of shepherdesses and garden gods. Poetry, he believed, should have moral and historical truth as its theme, it should be concerned with ordinary subjects that interest ordinary people; it should use not classical imagery but themes drawn from medieval and modern history. For Manzoni classicism and romanticism are opposed as Paganism and Christianity are. But here it is important to stress a point on which Manzoni was at variance with the French and German romantics. For him the antithesis Christianity-Paganism equals the antithesis Truth-Falsehood. In Christianity Manzoni saw *il vero*, and hence by romanticism he meant an attitude that nowadays we should probably call realism.

On this point a comparison with Stendhal is interesting, for Stendhal, too, was in an anomalous situation regarding romanticism. As Mr Martin Turnell has pointed out, 'Stendhal did not scruple to use the romantic stock in trade of scaling ladders, lovers concealed in cupboards, log cabins and the rest, but the tone of his work is unromantic and in the seduction of Mathilde de la Mole it becomes decidedly anti-romantic.[1]'

Manzoni occupied a central position in the romantic movement in Italy; he used all the romantic stage props, yet fundamentally he was not a romantic in the usual sense. He rejoined the great tradition of the European novel in his own unique and peculiarly Italian way.

[1] *The Novel in France*, p. 14.

BIOGRAPHICAL NOTES

1785 Manzoni born in Milan
1805 Departure for Paris
1805 *In Morte di Carlo Imbonati*
1808 Marriage to Henriette Blondel
1809 *Urania*
1810 Manzoni's conversion
1812–1817 *Inni Sacri*
1819 *Osservazioni sulla Morale Cattolica*
1820 *Il Conte di Carmagnola*
1821 *Marzo 1821* (published much later)
1821 *Il Cinque Maggio*
1822 *Adelchi*
1823 *Lettre à M. Chauvet*
1823 Letter to the Marchese D'Azeglio on romanticism
1827 *I Promessi Sposi*
1833 Death of Henriette
1840–1842 Revised, definitive edition of *I Promessi Sposi*
1850 *Del Romanzo Storico*
1850 *Dell' Invenzione*
1862 *Dell' Unita della Lingua*
1862–1868 *La Rivoluzione Francese del 1789 e la Rivoluzione Italiana del 1859* (unfinished)
1873 Death of Manzoni

BIBLIOGRAPHICAL NOTES

There is very little about Alessandro Manzoni in print in English. The reader may obtain *The Linguistic Writings of Alessandro Manzoni* by B. Reynolds. *Scrutiny* (Cambridge) published an article entitled *The Significance of Manzoni's Promessi Sposi* by D. A. Traversi in 1940. I have also seen *Alessandro Manzoni* by Professor A. P. d'Entrèves (British Academy Lecture, Vol. XXXV of the Proceedings of the British Academy). There is an excellent *Biographical Study of Manzoni* by Mr Archibald Colquhoun appended to his translation of *I Promessi Sposi*.

I Promessi Sposi has appeared in various abridged or bowdlerized English versions since 1828. The only complete translation in modern English is by Mr Colquhoun. It was published under the title *The Betrothed* in 1951 by J. M. Dent and Sons Ltd., in London, and by E. P. Dutton and Co. Inc. in New York. This translation is based on the Italian edition of Professors M. Barbi and E. Ghisalberti which was published by the *Casa del Manzoni* in 1942.

Italian editions of Manzoni's works, with commentaries and without, are very numerous. *I Promessi Sposi* has appeared in five hundred editions since its original publication. The bibliography concerning Manzoni is enormous, almost rivaling that of Dante. It covers every aspect, from his personal habits to *minutiae* of his style. Amongst modern works I might mention *Alessandro Manzoni* by Benedetto Croce (Bari 1930), *La Vita Religiosa di Alessandro Manzoni* by Francesco Ruffini (Bari 1931), *Alessandro Manzoni il Pensatore ed il Poeta* by A. Galletti (Milan 1927), *Manzoni* by Luigi Tonelli (third edition, Milan 1935), *Colloqui col Manzoni* by Umberto Calosso (Bari 1948), *A. Manzoni* by Attilio Momigliano (Messina 1933). The article on Manzoni in the Italian Encyclopedia is also by Attilio Momigliano.

Every history of Italian literature gives Manzoni his due position as one of the supreme writers of the last two centuries. Few living critics or essayists of standing have failed to write about Manzoni at one time or another.